THE
SMOOTHIE
RECIPE BOOK

SMOOTHIES FOR WEIGHT LOSS *and* **SMOOTHIES FOR GOOD HEALTH**

D0950394

Mendocino Press

CONTENTS

INTRODUCTION

Fruits and vegetables naturally contain many of the nutrients people need to survive and keep healthy. The concept of drinking smoothies and juices to maintain good health and cure many ailments has been around for centuries, but only recently has it gained popularity in Western civilization. There are as many different purposes for incorporating smoothies into your diet as there are ingredients to use in them. Some of these uses include:

- Anti-aging
- Diabetes control
- Disease prevention
- Healthy skin
- Increased cognitive function
- Meal replacement
- Weight loss

Though many people choose to extract the juice from the pulp, especially if they wish to detoxify, there are definite health advantages to drinking smoothies. Throughout the following pages you'll discover many of the ways these fiber-rich, low-calorie foods can help you achieve better health, but first, let's define what exactly a smoothie is.

Strictly speaking, a smoothie is a concoction created by blending the pulp, juice, and often the skins of fruits and vegetables into a soup or drink that is relatively smooth and requires little chewing. While purists add nothing except water to their smoothies, others may choose to add supplements or flavoring agents, such as protein powder, yogurt, milk, nuts, or seeds.

In the interest of giving you as many options as possible, this collection includes recipes of all kinds so you can choose for yourself. If a particular recipe that contains extra "stuff" sounds good to you, but you'd prefer to keep it pure, just omit those ingredients. The opposite is also true: If you'd like to add something to a particular recipe, feel free to do so. After all, it's your health and, therefore, your decision.

Now, it's time to talk smoothies!

1

BREAKFAST SMOOTHIES

S kipping breakfast may seem like a great way to cut calories and catch a few extra z's in the morning, but you're not helping your health or your weight-loss efforts. In fact, failing to eat a healthful morning meal has been linked to obesity, diabetes, mineral deficiencies, and a host of other health issues. On the other hand, people who eat a nutritious breakfast tend be healthier, more productive, and demonstrate superior mental clarity.

Those in the know postulate that there are several reasons why people who eat breakfast are healthier than those who don't.

- By eating early in the day, your body doesn't go into starvation mode and begin storing fat.
- People who skip meals are famished by the time they actually eat and therefore tend to overindulge.
- Those who eat a healthful breakfast tend to eat healthier foods and consequently consume fewer calories throughout the rest of the day.
- Eating healthful foods regularly throughout the day keeps your insulin levels stable.
- People who skip breakfast tend to eat more sugary foods and snack more often than people who don't.

However, not all breakfasts are created equal. People who eat large, heavy breakfasts such as omelets stuffed with fatty meats and cheeses or carb-filled pancakes and waffles tend to eat more calories at every meal throughout the day than their banana-grabbing counterparts. As a matter of fact, breakfast doesn't have to be a big meal for you to reap the health benefits. The important part is to "break the fast" between supper and lunch so that your body isn't deprived of nutrition for any longer than necessary.

Ideally, you should shoot for a breakfast that's high in protein, nutrients, good carbs, and healthful fats. Though they're tempting, avoid donuts, sugary muffins, and fast-food biscuits—these are packed with bad fats, empty simple carbs that suppress the sensation of fullness and can cause you to crave more sugar. If you don't have the time to sit down and eat a meal, a smoothie is a great, healthful alternative to fast foods or junk foods. In the pages to come, you'll find recipes that are both delicious and satisfying. Feel free to experiment with ingredients, and most important, have fun!

Pumpkin Juice

Packed with omega-3s and an army of antioxidants led by vitamin A, this smoothie has everything you need to get you through the day, and its rich, smooth flavor will remind you of fall. Blend it with ice for a refreshing, midsummer treat, or stick to the milk for a comforting winter pick-me-up.

- 1 sweet potato
- 1 carrot
- 1/2 cup pumpkin
- 1/4 avocado, pitted and peeled

- 1/2 cup almond milk, soy milk, or skim milk
- 1/8 teaspoon cinnamon (optional)

Cut the sweet potato into 1-inch pieces.

Juice the carrots and sweet potatoes first, followed by the pumpkin. You may enjoy adding cinnamon to this juice as well to give it a bit of spice.

Yield: About 3 cups.

Strawberry Banana Smoothie

This smoothie is a fresh and fruity way to start your day. The strawberries deliver vitamin A and the pomegranate does everything from actually stopping cancer to cleaning your teeth. Add in the potassium and vitamins from the banana along with the chlorophyll and other goodies from the cucumber, and you're nutritionally ready to start the day!

- 6 strawberries, capped
- 1 banana, peeled
- Seeds from 1 pomegranate
- 1 cucumber, quartered

Add all the ingredients to your blender, and puree. You'll get the benefit from the fiber and the nutrients in the skins as well! If needed, add a little water for a drinkable consistency.

Yield: About 2 cups.

Berry Melon Blast

This smoothie delivers a fruity blast of antioxidants, vitamins, and minerals that start your day right. The cucumber cuts the sweetness, but the flavors of the melon and berries really shine through.

- 6 medium strawberries, capped
- 1/4 honeydew, peeled and seeded
- 1/2 cup blueberries
- 1 cucumber, quartered

Simply blend together. The cucumber does an excellent job of cutting down some of the sweet flavor and lightening up the smoothie.

Yield: About 3 cups.

Guavaloupe Goodie

The carrot greens will make it green, but the taste is refreshing and tropical. Guava's nutritional value is right up there with pomegranates and avocados, beneficial for everything from digestive ailments to weight loss and beautiful skin. Since it has a low glycemic load, it's a great strawberry/kiwi-flavored fruit for everyone!

- 1 guava, peeled
- 1/4 cantaloupe, peeled and seeded
- 1 carrot with greens
- 1/2 cup coconut milk

This glass of delicious nutrition is as easy to drink as it is to prepare. Just blend and enjoy. Simple and delicious.

Yield: About 3 cups.

Plum Melon Chiller

This is a wonderful juice for a hot summer day—when serving, remember to garnish with a sprig of mint for an extra summery touch. It's also excellent if you're suffering the aftereffects of a late night—all of the ingredients provide antioxidants and energy that will gear you up to face your day.

- 2 plums
- 1 cup watermelon
- 1 small cucumber, quartered

Blend the ingredients and drink immediately. There should be exactly enough for 1 serving. Just delicious!

Yield: About 2 cups.

The Dish on Plums

The Good: *Plums are a very useful ingredient for smoothing texture or sweetening without adding strong flavors. Rich in vitamins A, C, and K, they help your body absorb iron and fight cancer. Since they're chock full of fiber as well as vitamin C, they're great for maintaining a healthy digestive and immune system as well.*

The Bad: *The only downside to plums is that they are high in sugar. They have a fairly low glycemic load, but if you're watching calories or sugar intake, be sure to factor in your plums.*

Mega Omega Smoothie

Between the omega-3s offered by the avocado, and the proliferate amount of phenols, vitamins C and E, and trace minerals found in the entire smoothie, you can't get any more brain-healthful than this. It's mildly sweet and full of good fiber and healthful carbs, so drink this for breakfast or to get you through that midmorning or late-afternoon brain slump.

- 1 avocado, pitted and peeled
- 1 mango, pitted and peeled
- Pinch cilantro
- 1/2 lime, peeled
- 1/2 cup strawberries, capped
- 1/4 cup water

Add all ingredients to your blender, and puree until it reaches the desired consistency. Since there are no flavors to hide, you may want to leave this one a bit chunky to get the satisfaction of chewing. Enjoy!

Yield: About 2 cups.

Veggie Boost

This is a vibrant, "green-tasting" drink with a mild, peppery flavor from the fennel, and the herbal goodness of basil. The cucumber helps to lighten it up and make this nutritional powerhouse delicious! Between all the healthful ingredients, you're getting just about every vitamin and mineral that vegetables have to offer, so drink up!

- 1/2 cup water
- 2 cups spinach
- 3 basil leaves
- 6 Brussels sprouts
- 1/4 fennel bulb
- 1 cucumber, quartered

Blend the water, spinach, basil, and Brussels sprouts, pulsing until they're in small chunks. Next, blend the fennel and the cucumber. If you'd like, add some black pepper, a pinch of sea salt, or maybe even a jalapeño.

Yield: About 2 cups.

Hangover Juice

Magnesium, vitamin C, and calcium do wonders for curing that nasty, day-after headache. You're probably dehydrated as well, so drink a big glass of water with this.

- 1 cup cauliflower
- 1 cup broccoli florets
- 1 apple, cored and quartered
- 1 orange, peeled

Blend the vegetables first, then the fruits. Drink on your way to work, and you'll be feeling better within the hour! If your hangover persists, drink another glass.

Yield: About 2 cups.

Apple Mint Juice

This smoothie is an odd color, but it's extremely flavorful. Lightly fruity with a minty undertone, this combination of phytonutrients and deliciously refreshing flavor is a great way to start your day. The fiber will keep you full for hours, too.

- 1 pear, cored and quartered
- 1 apple, cored and quartered
- 1 carrot with greens
- 2 kiwis, peeled
- 4 sprigs mint

Simply blend all ingredients together and enjoy!

Yield: About 3 cups.

The Dish on Kiwis

The Good: *Kiwis contains large amounts of chlorophyll and twice as much vitamin C as an orange.*

The Bad: *Much of the calories in a kiwi come from sugar, so you may want to use these sparingly as sweetening agents for high-fiber produce.*

Grape Berry Guava

*This fruity, berry-flavored concoction both looks and tastes delicious.
It's packed with disease-fighting antioxidants, tannins, vital minerals,
including magnesium and potassium, and even a few omega-3s.*

• 1 cup red grapes	• 1 cup raspberries
• 1 cup watermelon	• 1 guava, peeled

Blend all fruits together. If you'd like it creamy, add a splash or two
of almond or coconut milk.

Yield: About 2 cups.

Sweet Potato Pie

*This juice is delicious as well as nutritious—the beta-carotene alone makes
it well worth your efforts. It really does taste like sweet potato pie!*

• 1 small sweet potato	• 1/2 teaspoon cinnamon
• 1 carrot	• 1/4 teaspoon ground cloves
• 1/4 papaya, seeded and peeled	• 1 cup almond milk

Cut the sweet potato into 1-inch cubes.

Pulse the sweet potato, carrot, and papaya, then add the cinnamon
and cloves to the juice. Stir gently. If you enjoy its namesake, this
will likely be a favorite.

Yield: About 4 cups.

The Dish on Papaya

The Good: *Papayas have actually been shown to halt the growth of breast cancer and are suspected to fight other cancers as well, including prostate cancer. This is tentatively attributed to the high levels of carotenoids such as lycopene and beta-carotene. The potassium they contain is a good brain food, too.*

The Bad: *Papaya is an acquired taste, so if you're just starting to eat it, you may want to blend it with more familiar flavors, such as pineapple, banana, or cucumber.*

2

SMOOTHIES THAT NOURISH YOUR BRAIN

Your brain requires three things to function properly: sufficient exercise, plenty of sleep, and proper nutrition. Unfortunately, if you're one of the billions of people who follow the typical Western lifestyle, you probably aren't getting enough of any of these. The up side is that your brain is extremely good at making due for short periods of time, but it can't function optimally for too long without getting what it needs. As a matter of fact, many degenerative brain disorders are now being linked to poor dietary choices.

For most of human history, the functions of the brain have been a mystery, but in recent decades, scientists have begun to understand more clearly how it works. Just like a car, your brain functions only as long as you feed it the proper fuel. It requires specific nutrients to keep your thoughts flowing well and your memory operating efficiently. If you offer it a lifetime of garbage, it can literally wither up and quit working. Recent research is actually calling Alzheimer's disease "type 3 diabetes."

To completely oversimplify how sugar leads to Alzheimer's, let's take a basic look at how things work. Your pancreas produces insulin, which is what tells your cells to absorb blood sugar, aka glucose, that your brain uses for fuel. When the insulin sends signals to your cells too often, such as when you have too much sugar in your blood, your cells start ignoring the insulin. Now you're insulin resistant, and your brain isn't getting sufficient glucose to function properly. You begin to lose memory and cognitive skills, and Alzheimer's develops. This may be the "kindergarten" biology version, but you get the idea.

Some signs that your brain isn't getting the nutrients it needs include:

- Anxiety
- Brain fog
- Confusion
- Depression
- Poor memory

If you're experiencing any of these symptoms, you've likely written them off as simply part of living a stressful lifestyle and getting older—but this is not the case. Fortunately, smoothies are a great means of regaining quick nutrition so that your brain can begin to get rid of the garbage and start running on all eight cylinders again. Look for produce that contains brain-healthful omega-3s, B vitamins, and vitamins C, D, and E. Here are a few great recipes to help you get back on track to mental clarity and superhero brain function.

Cherry Berry Mint Julep

The more people learn about cherries, the more advantageous they turn out to be. They're heart healthful and have anti-inflammatory benefits excellent for disease prevention and arthritis treatment. This delightfully minty, berry-flavored juice will doubtless be a new favorite!

- 1 cup cherries, pitted
- 4 sprigs mint
- 1/2 small cucumber, quartered
- 1 cup raspberries
- 1 apple, cored and quartered

Blend all ingredients together. If the consistency is a bit thick, add 1/2 cup water or coconut water. The mint adds a nice touch to this smoothie.

Yield: About 2 cups.

The Thinking Beauty Juice

This veggie-flavored mix helps your brain in a variety of different ways. The antioxidants protect you from cognitive decline and help boost your memory, while other nutrients, such as omega-3s, promote good blood flow and enhance critical thinking skills.

- 1/2 sweet potato
- 2 cups spinach
- 1 clove garlic
- 1 carrot with greens
- 1/2 small cucumber, quartered
- 1/2 cup water

Cut the sweet potato into 1-inch cubes.

Pulse the spinach, garlic, and sweet potato first, then add the rest. The cucumber lightens the flavor a bit.

Yield: About 2 cups.

Mango Mint

This exotic, melon-berry-flavored smoothie is packed with beta-carotene, omega-3s, and other brain-boosting nutrients that will really help you think clearly. It tastes so delicious you'll never believe it's good for you!

- 1/2 mango, pitted and peeled
- 3 sprigs mint
- 1 cup pomegranate seeds
- 1/4 papaya, seeded and peeled
- 1/2 cup almond milk

Blend all ingredients together. Tropical and refreshing, this smoothie reminds you of an exotic vacation.

Yield: About 2 cups.

The Dish on Pomegranates

The Good: *Pomegranate seeds are a great source of antioxidants and anti-inflammatory properties that protect you from a host of illnesses, including cancer. There are also some indications that they may protect you from plaque buildup that contributes to Alzheimer's disease.*

The Bad: *Pomegranates tend to be expensive and can be difficult to find in many locations. The seeds are also a bit of a trick to extract until you get the hang of it.*

Berry-Berry Cherry Juice

The intense fruity and berry flavors of this smoothie are lightened up by the lemon and the cucumber. Meanwhile, the antioxidants, minerals, and phytonutrients it contains will kick your brain into high gear.

- 1 cup dark cherries, pitted
- 1 cup blueberries
- 1 cup raspberries
- 1/2 lemon, peeled
- 1 cucumber, quartered

Blend all ingredients together. The lemon slows down oxidation, so you can take this to work with you without worrying about losing nutritional value.

Yield: About 2 cups.

Blueberry Blast

Adults who drink blueberry juice tend to score better on cognitive tests, including memory and critical thinking, and blackberries are great for your noggin, too. Meanwhile, cucumbers add brain-healthful chlorophyll and lighten up the intense berry flavor of this drink.

- 1 cup blueberries
- 1 cup blackberries

- 1 cucumber, quartered

Blend all ingredients together. If you'd like to add even more brainpower while lending the smoothie a creamy, nutty flavor, add 1/2 cup almond milk.

Yield: About 2 cups.

The Dish on Blueberries

The Good: *You know about all the good antioxidants and nutrients in blueberries, but here's a fun fact: they help improve balance, coordination, and short-term memory in aging rats!*

The Bad: *Blueberries have a high sugar content, so if you're a diabetic or are just watching your sugar intake, cut down their quantity by mixing them with other high-fiber produce.*

Cherry Apple Chiller

Great for serving guests, this smoothie packs a nutritional punch that's hard to beat. Add the fact that it tastes fizzy and fruity, and you have a hit!

- 1 apple, cored and quartered
- 1 cup sour cherries, pitted
- 2 sprigs mint
- 2 ounces seltzer water

Blend the apple, cherries, and mint. Add the seltzer water to the smoothie, and pulse once or twice just to blend before pouring into the glass.

Yield: About 2 cups.

Great Minds Gazpacho

The rich variety of omega-3s, antioxidants, brain-healthful vitamins, and phytonutrients in this soup will give you a real boost. The zesty, green flavors blend well to remind you of a delicious salad or a tasty, veggie sauce. You can control the spice level by removing the seeds from the jalapeño or omitting it altogether, though it lends a nice note to the soup. If you'd rather take it to go, simply drink it as a smoothie.

- 1/2 cup water
- 2 cloves garlic, peeled
- 1 cucumber, quartered
- 1 avocado, pitted and peeled
- 1 green bell pepper, de-stemmed
- 1 medium jalapeño pepper, de-stemmed (optional)
- 1 medium zucchini, quartered
- 2 scallions
- Lime juice, for garnish

Add the water to your blender along with the garlic, cucumber, and avocado. Pulse a few times to cut them into smaller pieces, and then add the next few ingredients. Repeat until all ingredients are incorporated, then blend until smooth. Serve in a soup bowl and garnish with a full lime twist.

Yield: About 4 cups.

Focused Vitality Smoothie

The quercetin in apples has been shown to protect your brain from diseases such as Alzheimer's, and asparagus is packed with vitamins A, C, E, and K, plus chromium, a mineral that helps insulin transport glucose, your brain's fuel. The lettuce and grapes are nutritious as well, and add a pleasing, mild flavor to this fresh-tasting smoothie.

- 4 stalks asparagus tips, tender halves only
- 1 green apple, cored and quartered
- 1/2 cup water
- 2 cups romaine lettuce, chopped
- 1 cup green grapes

Add the asparagus, apple, and water to the blender, and pulse until it's into small chunks. Add the rest of the ingredients and puree.

Yield: About 2 cups.

Mental Monkey Wrench

The vitamin C, flavonoids, and healthful carbs in this smoothie will really help keep your head clear and your thoughts running smoothly. If you'd like an additional boost of omega-3s, throw in an avocado as well. You're going to love the fruity taste for breakfast or as a pre-workout snack.

- 1 cup green grapes
- 2 kiwis, peeled
- 1 banana, peeled

Toss the grapes, kiwis, and banana into your blender and puree.

Yield: About 2 cups.

Beachside Breakfast for Your Brain

Vitamin C is great for memory, and this smoothie delivers it in spades. Since the spinach throws in brain-friendly folate, plus vitamins E and K, your noggin will love this tropical-tasting brew as much as you do!

- 1/4 pineapple, peeled
- 1/4 cantaloupe, peeled and seeded
- 1 cup spinach
- 1 orange, peeled
- 1 cup pomegranate seeds

Cut the pineapple into 1-inch cubes.

Toss all of the ingredients into the blender and puree.

Yield: About 2 cups.

3

ALKALIZING SMOOTHIES: PROTECT YOUR BONES AND KIDNEYS

Though there's lots of hype about the importance of alkalizing your blood to prevent all kinds of diseases, for the most part, hype is exactly what it is. Under normal circumstances, dietary choices have little, if any, direct impact on your blood pH levels. Your body is alkaline by nature and has a pretty nifty system of checks and balances to keep your blood pH somewhere between 7.35 and 7.45. What you eat can affect the pH of your urine and other bodily fluids, however, and that can seriously impact your health.

Bones

It's a fact that foods vary in acidity and need to be adjusted by the body. Your body also creates acids that need to be neutralized just by performing basic activities such as breathing, exercising, and digesting food. If you eat the recommended daily allowance of fruits and vegetables, your body can neutralize about 50 mEq of acid—anything more than that and your body starts pulling calcium and other minerals from your bones to alkalize your blood.

Unfortunately, most people who live on a Western diet take in about 100 mEq of acid per day and eat far less than the daily recommended servings of produce. That means that on a daily basis, your body has to pull critical minerals from your bones just to keep you alive. On the other hand, increasing your fruit and vegetable intake will provide your body what it needs and preserve the strength of your bones, possibly helping you avoid such conditions as osteoporosis.

Kidney Stones

As mentioned above, whether or not you can alter the pH of your blood significantly with diet is debatable, but the pH levels of your urine and other bodily fluids *are* influenced by what you eat. When your body has to draw calcium from your bones and teeth to alkalize itself, that calcium can build up in your kidneys and cause painful kidney stones. This can largely be prevented by eating enough alkalizing foods.

Now that you understand a few of the reasons why it's so important to eat plenty of fruits and vegetables, it's pretty obvious how adding a smoothie or two to your daily diet can help keep you alkalized and healthy. Some foods are more alkalizing than others, and you'll find a variety of smoothie recipes that use them to their best advantage in the following pages.

Orange Carrot Smoothie

Though most people think of oranges as acidic, they're actually alkalizing after they mingle with your stomach acid. Coconut water is also soothing to your digestive tract, while the beta-carotene in carrots is a great antioxidant boost. This smoothie tastes both fresh and a bit citrusy.

- 1 yellow beet
- 1 carrot with greens
- 1 orange, peeled
- 1/2 cup coconut water

Pulse the beet and the carrot, then add the orange and coconut water. *Yield: About 2 cups.*

The Dish on Coconut Water

The Good: *Coconut water is often used to treat diarrhea and other digestive issues because it's packed with enzymes and electrolytes. It's also sterile and has a near-perfect pH, and can thus be used in a pinch as a substitute for blood plasma.*

The Bad: *What makes coconut juice ideal for sports drinks actually makes it less so for people concerned about sugar and sodium intake, as this refreshing juice is relatively high in both.*

Potato Pineapple Potash

Potatoes are so alkalizing that they're frequently used alone to treat acne from the inside out. Pineapples, kiwis, and ginger are also extremely alkalizing, as well as delicious and good for digestion. The fruity, tropical taste of the kiwis and pineapple meld with the spicy ginger, and you'll never even know the potato is there.

- 1 red potato
- 1/4 pineapple, peeled
- 1/4 inch slice ginger
- 2 kiwis, peeled

Chop the red potato and pineapple into 1-inch cubes.

Pulse the potato and ginger, then add the pineapple and kiwi. If you feel it's needed, add 1/4 cup water or organic apple juice.

Yield: About 2 cups.

Cranberry Lemonade

Though cranberries are acidic, this is balanced by the alkalizing power of the lemons. The antimicrobial effects of the cranberries help your kidneys fight off stones caused by acidic pH levels. Plus, everybody loves lemonade!

- 1 cup cranberries
- 2 lemons, peeled
- 3 cups water

Light and refreshing, this smoothie is made by simply blending the cranberries and lemons, then adding the water. The lemons prevent oxidation, so go ahead and make multiple servings, even if you won't be drinking them right away—they won't lose their nutritional value. Enjoy!

Yield: About 4 cups.

Mint Magic

Greens are known to be alkalizing, and the benefits of lemons were previously discussed. This drink is great for a hot, summer afternoon, because it's light and refreshing, and the mint will soothe your digestive system.

- 1 cucumber, quartered
- 1/2 bunch fresh parsley
- 1/2 lemon, peeled
- 1 cup alfalfa sprouts
- 4 sprigs fresh mint

Blend all ingredients together and enjoy.

Yield: About 2 cups.

Green Restorative

You may as well call garlic and cabbage the equalizing twins, as they're simultaneously beneficial for your blood and your circulation. This smoothie has a fairly green flavor so you may want to toss in an apple or cucumber.

- 1 cup broccoli florets
- 2 stalks celery
- 2 cups spinach
- 1 clove garlic, peeled
- 1/4 head cabbage
- 1 cup water

Blend all ingredients together.

Yield: 3 cups.

Red Refresher

This is delicious, refreshing, and fabulous for you—not to mention it has a beautiful color!

- 1 beet
- 1 cup pomegranate seeds (or 1 cup cranberries)
- 1 cup watermelon
- 1/2 lime, peeled

Pulse the beet first, and then toss in the rest. Blend and enjoy.

Yield: About 2 cups.

Potato Melon Nectar

This smoothie contains a ton of the minerals, such as calcium, that your body needs to maintain proper pH. It tastes great, too, with a refreshing, slightly sweet, melony flavor.

- 1 small sweet potato
- 1 small white potato
- 1/4 cantaloupe, peeled and seeded
- 1/4 cucumber, quartered

Chop the sweet potato and white potato into 1-inch cubes.

Pulse the potatoes, then add the rest of the ingredients. This one's refreshing as well as good for your skin.

Yield: About 3 cups.

The Green Carrot

Greens contain the calcium your body needs to maintain alkalinity, and carrots are rich in minerals. This drink has a garden-green taste, with a touch of sweet flavor from the carrot.

- 1 cup broccoli florets
- 1 carrot with greens
- 2 cups spinach
- 6 Brussels sprouts
- 1 cup water

Pulse all vegetables first, then add water and blend. For a snappy kick, try adding some jalapeño pepper.

Yield: About 3 cups.

Bugs' Juice

It doesn't get any more alkalizing than this, and all of these greens offer calcium and minerals to keep your bones and teeth strong. The watercress lends a peppery flavor, while the carrots add a bit of sweetness.

- 1 whole watercress
- 1 cup spinach
- 1 cup broccoli florets
- 1 carrot with greens
- 1 cup water

Pulse the watercress, spinach, and broccoli first. Finish by blending it all together.

Yield: About 2 cups.

Beta to C You with Smoothie

Limes are one of the most alkalizing foods you can eat, and the calcium and minerals provided by the carrots and greens make this excellent for your pH as well. The smoothie has a rich, green taste, lightened and sweetened by the lime, carrot, and cucumber.

- 2 kale leaves
- 1 cup spinach
- 1 lime, peeled
- 1 green bell pepper, de-stemmed
- 1 cucumber, quartered
- 1 carrot with greens

Pulse the kale, spinach, and lime. Next, add the pepper, cucumber, and carrot. You may want to add 1/2 cup water to the smoothie to loosen it up a bit.

Yield: About 3 cups.

The Dish on Limes

The Good: *In addition to being packed with vitamin C, limes are also extremely alkalizing to your body, despite the high citric acid content. The citric acid in limes is also great for stimulating weight loss, and it's a great antioxidant, so it helps you fight disease.*

The Bad: *Though it's alkalizing once it hits your stomach, the acid in the limes can damage the surface of your teeth, so be sure to rinse your mouth after drinking anything containing lime juice. Limes also have a significant amount of carbohydrates from fruit sugars, so tread carefully if you're monitoring your sugar intake.*

4

ANTI-AGING SMOOTHIES

Anti-aging research is a multibillion-dollar industry, and as baby boomers start to surpass middle age and head into their golden years, the search for youth-restoring elixirs and techniques to stay youthful is progressing at a frenzied pace. What the research is finding is nothing short of incredible. Many of the diseases and conditions that people have come to accept as unavoidable effects of aging are actually caused by poor diets, environmental toxins, lack of proper exercise, or other controllable factors.

One of the best ways to combat both age-related diseases and the physical signs of aging is to follow a healthful diet rich in fruits and vegetables. Try to eat a variety of colors, because each color group offers different vitamins and phytonutrients. Shoot especially for greens, reds, and purples, because they're the richest in free radical-fighting antioxidants. Get a good daily dose of omega-3 fatty acids as well. They're great for your brain, your skin, your heart, and just about every other part of you, and can be found in nuts, fish, seafood, and produce such as avocados and leafy greens.

Here are a few terrific smoothie recipes that will help keep you looking and feeling young!

Plum Yummy

Plums are an anti-aging superfood; they are proven to help with iron absorption, and the vitamin C gives a nice boost to your immune system. Finally, the antioxidants in this smoothie help fight cancer as well as wrinkles and other signs of aging.

- 1/2 cup water
- 1 plum, pitted
- 2 kiwis, peeled
- 2 cups spinach
- 6 mint leaves, plus 1 for garnish
- 1 teaspoon ginger, grated

Add the water, plum, and kiwis to your blender, and pulse for a few seconds. Add the spinach, mint, and ginger, and puree. Garnish with a mint leaf and enjoy!

Yield: About 2 cups.

The Dish on Ginger

The Good: *Ginger has been used for centuries as a digestive aid and to relieve symptoms of arthritis. Its anti-inflammatory properties also help protect you from heart disease, cancer, and other conditions. In addition, the gingerol it contains has actually been proven to cause cell death in ovarian cancer cells.*

The Bad: *Ginger has a strong flavor and is difficult to cut. Use it sparingly until you learn how much is enough.*

Youthful Italiana

This delicious smoothie is reminiscent of spaghetti sauce. The beta-carotene in the tomatoes, kale, and pepper is great for your eyes, and the antioxidants in all of the ingredients help fight wrinkles. Garlic is known to fight off disease, and basil is rich in calcium. Kale is also a good source of brain-healthful omega-3s.

- 1 tomato
- 1 clove garlic
- 1 green bell pepper, de-stemmed
- 3 basil leaves
- 2 kale leaves

If this smoothie is a bit too thick, just add water. It can work equally well for lunch or dinner. As a matter of fact, if you'd like to leave it a bit thick, it's great as a chilled soup.

Yield: About 2 cups.

Super Berry Freshee

The berries in this smoothie provide antioxidants that help maintain memory and brain function while fighting off wrinkles and disease. Bananas are a great source of potassium and vitamin B6, both of which offer valuable anti-aging benefits. Finally, the resveratrol and other nutrients in the grapes add a final age-fighting punch. This smoothie tastes fresh and delicious, too.

- 1 banana, peeled
- 5 strawberries, capped, plus 1 strawberry for garnish
- 1/4 cup blueberries
- 4 kiwis, peeled
- 1 small cucumber, quartered
- 1/4 cup water

Toss all ingredients in your blender and puree until smooth. Pour into glass and garnish with a strawberry.

Yield: About 4 cups.

Apple of Popeye's Eye

This one's about as green as it gets. The antioxidants, vitamin A, calcium, and folate in this smoothie make it an anti-aging powerhouse, promoting good vision, brain health, and urinary tract health, just to name a few of its benefits. After drinking this smoothie, you'll feel like a spring chicken!

- 1 green apple, cored and quartered
- 6 asparagus tips
- 2 cups spinach
- 1 cucumber, quartered
- 1/2 cup water

Add the apple and asparagus to the blender, and pulse until they are in chunks. Toss in the remaining ingredients, and puree until it reaches the desired texture. This one may be a little chewy and will keep you full for hours.

Yield: About 3 1/2–4 cups.

The Mr. Ed Special

It's no wonder horses love this stuff: packed with vitamins, antioxidants, and minerals that help fight cancer, promote good eyesight and digestion, and help keep you mentally sharp, it's a glass of amazing!

- 1 carrot with greens
- 1 green apple, cored and quartered
- 1/2 cup water
- 1 small cucumber, quartered
- 6 mint leaves

Blend the carrot, apple, and water on the "chop" setting, then toss in the cucumber and mint leaves. Puree to the consistency you prefer.

Yield: About 2 cups.

Cranberry Watermelon Smoothie

Bursting with phytonutrients and minerals, this hydrating drink is good for everything from kidney health to cancer prevention. The watermelon makes it really juicy and just a bit sweet, while the beet adds its own mild but distinctive flavor. The deep red color is visually appealing, too.

- 1 beet, with or without greens
- 1 cup cranberries
- 1 cup watermelon
- 1/2 cup water

Pulse the beet first, then add the berries. Finish up with the watermelon and water, and enjoy.

Yield: About 2 cups.

Beeting Wrinkles

Beets contain an eclectic collection of antioxidants, including betalain, beta-carotene, and vitamin C, making this nutritious as well as tasty and beautiful. This smoothie will help you fight aging on all fronts, from disease prevention to fighting wrinkles. The beets also add a mildly sweet flavor.

- 1 small sweet potato
- 1 beet, with or without greens
- 1 carrot with greens
- 1 cucumber, quartered

Cut the sweet potato into 1-inch cubes.

Pulse your sweet potato and beet first, then add the carrot and cucumber. Once you get past the fact that the taste doesn't match the color, you'll really enjoy this juice!

Yield: About 3 cups.

Antioxidant Punch

This is a cancer-preventing, wrinkle-fighting heavyweight with a light, mildly fruity flavor.

- 2 stalks celery
- 2 broccoli florets
- 1 cup blueberries
- 1 banana, peeled
- 1 cucumber, quartered

Pulse the celery and broccoli, then add the rest of the ingredients. Blend and enjoy!

Yield: About 2 cups.

The Dish on Broccoli

The Good: *Broccoli is high in antioxidant vitamins A and C, folic acid, calcium, and phytochemicals that can help you lose weight, look younger, and avoid disease.*

The Bad: *Raw broccoli contains goitrogens that can interfere with thyroid function if you already have issues, so if you have a history of thyroid concerns, you may want to lightly steam your broccoli before eating it.*

Fine Line Wine

This is a fantastic smoothie for breakfast—start your day with an antioxidant wallop!

- 1/2 cup blueberries
- 1/2 cup blackberries
- 1/2 cup raspberries
- 1/2 cup strawberries, capped
- 1 apple, cored and quartered
- 1/2 cup red grapes

This one's easy—just blend and enjoy.

Yield: About 2 cups.

Looking Berry Young Smoothie

Antioxidants, such as vitamins A and C, in this smoothie help destroy wrinkle-causing, disease-feeding free radicals, while the probiotics in the yogurt help you maintain good digestive health. It tastes "berry" delicious, too!

- 1 cup blueberries
- 1 cup raspberries
- 1 cup strawberries, capped
- 1 cup pomegranate seeds
- 1/2 cup plain yogurt

Blend all ingredients together and enjoy!

Yield: About 2 cups.

5

ANTIOXIDANT SMOOTHIES

B efore you can understand how important antioxidants are to your body, you first need to understand what they do. In a nutshell, they do exactly what their name implies: they prevent oxidization in your body caused by free radicals. Free radicals are cells that have lost an electron and become unstable. In an attempt to become stable again, they steal electrons from healthy cells, thus creating another free radical.

Healthy molecules don't usually lose their electrons, but some-times it happens to weak molecules during respiration or other bodily functions. Sometimes your body has these to attach to harm-ful bacteria and other pathogens in an attempt to neutralize them and carry them from your body. Finally, free radicals can be created by contact with environmental toxins such as pollution, UVA rays, cigarettes, and pesticides.

The very least free radicals will do is make your skin and hair dull and start the outward signs of aging, such as wrinkles and sun spots. In more dire scenarios, they can cause heart disease, cancer, and eventual death. Antioxidants are the happy little nutrients that bounce around sharing their electrons with free radicals, and therefore neutralizing them. Since they are stable in either form, there is no danger of the antioxidant becoming a free radical itself.

All fruits and vegetables are rich in antioxidants, but watch especially for ones rich in the antioxidant vitamins A, C, and E. If you're ready to start blending up some smoothies that will help you get bright skin and beautiful hair while fighting off wrinkles and disease, then read on!

Antioxidant Ale

This is a great juice to start off your day. It's rich in antioxidants and contains fruit that will give you that nice energy pop.

- 1/2 sweet potato
- 1/2 cup raspberries
- 1/2 cup orange, peeled
- 4 strawberries, capped
- 1/2 cucumber, quartered
- 4 mint sprigs (optional)

Cut the sweet potato into 1-inch chunks.

Add all ingredients and blend. The antioxidant punch in this juice is absolutely out of this world, and the flavor is truly yummy!

Yield: About 2 cups.

The Dish on Sweet Potatoes

The Good: *Sweet potatoes are high in antioxidant vitamins C and E, and the cancer-fighting, vision-preserving carotenoid, beta-carotene. They're also a good source of fiber, manganese, potassium, and B6, which makes them extremely good for your heart.*

The Bad: *Many of the nutrients in sweet potatoes are concentrated in the skin, so don't peel them. To avoid pesticides, be sure to scrub them extremely well. Of course, organic is best.*

SuperShake

Speaking of antioxidants, this smoothie is a powerhouse of anti-aging, disease-fighting superstars. If you want to tone it down a bit, toss in a couple of tomatoes or cucumbers.

- 1 clove garlic
- 1/4 head cabbage
- 1 kale leaf
- 1 beet
- 1 carrot
- 1 stalk celery
- 1 cup water

Add all ingredients and blend. If you'd like, add a pinch or two of sea salt for flavor and a mineral boost, or perhaps cayenne for the extra antioxidant pop from the capsaicin.

Yield: About 3 cups.

Thanksgiving in a Glass

Though this tastes so good you won't believe it's good for you, rest assured that it is! The spices are amazing antioxidants, and the squash and pumpkin contain all the vitamins necessary for disease prevention. It's also advantageous for your eyes, so drink up!

- 1 apple, cored and quartered
- 1 cup pumpkin
- 1 small cucumber, quartered
- 1 carrot
- 1/2 teaspoon ground cloves
- 1/2 teaspoon ground cinnamon

Add the produce to your blender in the order listed. When blended, add the spices to your glass, stir, and enjoy!

Yield: About 2 cups.

Arugula Pepper Punch

This peppery drink is packed full of chlorophyll, cancer-fighting antioxidants, vitamins, and minerals. It also has a light, peppery flavor that's perfect for lunchtime.

- 1 cup arugula
- 1/2 whole watercress
- 1 stalk celery
- 1/2 pound lemongrass
- 1 green bell pepper, de-stemmed
- 1/2 teaspoon prepared horseradish

Blend all ingredients together and enjoy!

Yield: About 2 cups.

Rabbit Reduction

This delivers a huge serving of nutrients, including heart-healthful chlorophyll. It's also packed with indispensable minerals, like calcium, and has a nice light, green flavor that matches its color.

- 1 carrot with greens
- 1 apple, cored and quartered
- 1 cucumber, quartered
- 2 kale leaves

Blend all ingredients together and enjoy.

Yield: About 2 cups.

Salsa Soup Puree

The health benefits of this delicious, spicy, salsa-flavored puree are out of this world. It includes numerous, cancer-preventing antioxidants, and the lycopene in tomatoes helps keep your vision healthy. Capsaicin in the jalapeño pepper and vitamin C in the lime and garlic help you avoid colds and maintain healthy digestion. To control the spiciness, simply remove the pepper seeds.

- 1 tomato, cored
- 1 cucumber, quartered
- 1 green bell pepper, de-stemmed
- 1 jalapeño pepper, de-stemmed
- 2 cloves garlic
- 1/2 lime, peeled
- 3 medium sprigs cilantro
- 1 green onion
- Parsley, for garnish
- 1 teaspoon chopped scallions, for garnish

Combine all ingredients in your blender, and blend until smooth. Serve in a soup bowl, and garnish with a sprig of parsley and chopped scallions.

Yield: About 3 cups.

Plumarita Punch

This drink helps your body do everything from cure ulcers to prevent cancer. Plums also promote iron absorption. This delicious punch is fruity and zesty but not overwhelmingly sweet—you may not even notice the spinach and the cabbage.

- 1 plum, seeded
- 1 green apple, cored and quartered
- 2 cups spinach
- 1 cup cabbage
- 1/2 lime, peeled

Simply puree everything together in your blender. If you'd like to have it a bit thinner, add 1/4 cup water.

Yield: About 2 1/2–3 cups.

South of the Border Smoothie

Avocados are rich in omega-3 fatty acids, which help you maintain brain health as well as fight cancer, depression, wrinkles, and a host of other diseases. Vitamins A and C are both powerful antioxidants, and this smoothie contains a ton of each. Reminiscent of salsa because of the tomatoes and cilantro, this smoothie is both filling and delicious.

- 1 tomato
- 1 avocado, pitted and peeled
- 1 green onion
- 1 small sprig cilantro
- 1/2 lime, peeled

Blend everything together, adding 1/4 cup water if you'd like for it to be thinner.

Yield: About 2 cups.

Fruity Vitality Smoothie

Cantaloupe is incredible for your immune system, and kiwis protect the DNA in the nucleus of your cells. The raspberries are packed with disease-fighting antioxidants, and the iron, magnesium, and calcium in the spinach are great for you, too. This smoothie a bit sweet and tart, and you may not even notice the spinach except as a background note.

- 1/4 cantaloupe, peeled and seeded
- 2 kiwis, peeled
- 1 cup raspberries
- 2 cups spinach

The cantaloupe and kiwis should provide plenty of juice to make the smoothie, but if you'd prefer it thinner, just add a bit of water. Blend all ingredients together and enjoy!

Yield: About 3 cups.

The Dish on Cantaloupe

The Good: *Cantaloupes are a great source of vitamins A and C. They contain other free radical-fighting antioxidants and promote a healthy immune system as well. The beta-carotene helps keep your eyes healthy.*

The Bad: *Cantaloupe contains significant amounts of sugar, and as they ripen, get even sweeter. Mix with foods that are high in fiber and low in sugar to help combat sugar spikes.*

Immunity Endurance Smoothie

This well-balanced smoothie has a touch of sweet that combines nicely with the savory broccoli flavor. Among many other health benefits, this smoothie really gives your immune system a boost.

- 2 cups broccoli florets
- 1 cucumber, quartered
- 3 stalks celery
- 1 carrot
- 1 apple, cored and quartered
- 1/2 cup water

Starting with the broccoli, pulse into small pieces, then slowly add the other ingredients and puree.

Yield: About 3 cups.

6

CLEANSING SMOOTHIES

There are several different methods to clean out your system. Some people like to cleanse with smoothies for a day or two just to give their bodies a break from fats, heavy protein, and other difficult-to-digest foodstuffs or to ease into a more intense juice fast. A major benefit of a cleanse lasting only a few days is that you don't have time to get sick of living on just smoothies or juice. One of the downsides, though, especially if you're drinking fiber-filled smoothies, is that your system can't really clean itself out thoroughly in less than three days.

If you'd like to completely cleanse your digestive tract of accumulated toxins, parasites, and fecal matter, you may want to consider a smoothie cleanse that lasts three days at the very minimum—it takes that long for that steak that you ate today to get completely through your system, so anything shorter won't be as effective.

Another good option if you'd like to detoxify as well as cleanse is to alternate between smoothies and juices. Drink smoothies for a few days; then drink only juice for at least three days. The main difference between the two is that juices don't have the fiber in them.

Since your digestive tract doesn't have to extract the nutrients from the pulp, the nutrients are all absorbed in just a few minutes, and your body can use the extra energy to heal and cleanse your body of toxins and other harmful substances.

However, all smoothies are great for cleaning out your digestive system, and you'll find a few below particularly suited to the task.

Apple Detox

This recipe is light and delicious but also a powerhouse of cleansing. Because of the high sugar content, this is a great breakfast juice to get you started on your day.

- 1 green apple, cored and quartered
- 2 springs mint
- 1/2 lemon, peeled
- 1 orange, peeled
- 1/2 cucumber, quartered

Just toss it all in and hit puree!

Yield: About 2 cups.

Dandy-Kale Delight

Though this recipe calls for dandelion greens, any greens will do—they're rich in minerals that help your body heal. This definitely has a green taste, so if you'd like to sweeten it up while adding even more antioxidants, add another apple.

- 2 cups dandelion greens
- 2 kale leaves
- 1 apple, cored and quartered
- 1 cucumber, quartered
- 3 stalks celery

The rich green color of this drink gives you a sense of the healing benefits contained within. Mix all ingredients in the blender in the order listed.

Yield: About 2 cups.

Italian Fennel Cleanse

This smoothie is rich in calcium, vitamin C, and other valuable nutrients that your body needs to heal. Strongly flavored, it's slightly reminiscent of a pesto sauce.

- 1 clove garlic, peeled
- 1/4 bulb fennel with greens
- 2 kale leaves
- 8 basil leaves
- 1 tomato, cored
- 1 cucumber, quartered
- 1/2 lemon, peeled

Blend all ingredients. The fennel adds a peppery flair, and the lemon juice freshens it up, while all the ingredients work together to detoxify.

Yield: About 3 cups.

The Dish on Garlic

The Good: *Garlic is packed with so many nutrients, anti-inflammatory properties, antibacterials, and antioxidants, it's a wonder it doesn't explode right out of the bulb! It's proven to prevent many types of cancer, is a great digestive aid, and gives your immune system a nice boost.*

The Bad: *Garlic is pungent, and the smell tends to linger. There are no health "downsides." If you need to get the smell of garlic off your hands, rub them with a stainless steel spoon. This works so well you can actually buy stainless steel bars of "soap."*

The Delicious Green Cleanse

This beautiful, green drink is as good for you as it looks. Fortunately, it also tastes refreshing and pleasant while it works hard to fight diseases and detoxify your body.

- 1 green bell pepper, de-stemmed
- 1 cup broccoli florets
- 1 cucumber, quartered
- 1/4 head cabbage

Blend all greens together in the order listed. If you feel it tastes too rich, add a bit more cucumber. All of these ingredients work well independently as detoxifiers, but together they create a real powerhouse.

Yield: About 2 cups.

The Dish on Green Bell Peppers

The Good: *In addition to all of the other impressive health benefits, green peppers have about twice the vitamin C as an orange.*

The Bad: *Peppers tend to make some people a bit gassy, so add them slowly until your body gets accustomed to eating them.*

Popeye's Pride

This rich green drink will really give your body a detoxifying boost. The lemon and celery work to cleanse your system, while lending a refreshing taste to the spinach.

- 2 cups spinach
- 1/2 lemon, peeled
- 1 sprig parsley
- 2 stalks celery

Just blend all ingredients together until smooth.

Yield: About 2 cups.

Cleansing Cocktail

Cabbage is traditionally used as a cleanser for your digestive tract. If you like spice, throw in a jalapeño pepper for a fiesta in a glass!

- 5 broccoli florets
- 2 green bell peppers, de-stemmed
- 1/4 head green cabbage
- 1/2 cup water
- 2 tomatoes

Pulse the broccoli first, then the peppers. Next, throw in the cabbage and water, and finally the tomatoes.

Yield: About 3 cups.

Liven Up Your Liver Juice

Even the pretty color of this one will make your liver smile. This smoothie is packed with as much flavor as nutritional value, and will keep you coming back for more.

- 1 beet with greens
- 1 carrot with greens
- 1 apple, cored and quartered
- 1 inch slice ginger
- 1/2 cup water
- 1/4 teaspoon cinnamon

Blend all of the ingredients together except the cinnamon. Stir in the cinnamon.

Yield: About 2 cups.

Antioxidants Plus

This delicious vegetable-flavored drink tastes like that veggie blend that you buy in the store, only better. It's packed with age-defying, disease-fighting antioxidants, too.

- 1/2 clove garlic, peeled
- 1 celery stalk
- 1 green bell pepper, de-stemmed
- 1 carrot
- 1/8 head cabbage
- 6 kale leaves
- 1 cup spinach
- 1 tomato

Blend all ingredients together. If you need more moisture, add 1/2 cup water.

Yield: About 2 cups.

Orange Pineapple Chili

Pineapple is excellent for digestion, and the vitamins and antioxidants in this drink help your body heal. The cayenne adds a nice, southwestern flair to this tropical delight.

- 1 orange, peeled
- 1/4 pineapple, peeled

- 2 carrots
- 1/2 teaspoon cayenne pepper

Blend all ingredients together. This is actually quite helpful for getting rid of a cold, too.

Yield: About 2 cups.

Sweet Spinach Carrot

The fiber in this smoothie will sweep the garbage out of your digestive tract, while the minerals and chlorophyll really aid in healing. You'll find the taste is slightly sweet, carroty, and enjoyable.

- 1/2 sweet potato
- 2 cups spinach

- 2 carrots
- 1 cup water or apple juice

Cut the sweet potato into 1-inch pieces.

Blend all ingredients together. You'll be surprised by the sweet flavor of this juice, even if the color may not be so pretty! (And it's excellent for cleaning your colon, too!)

Yield: About 2 cups.

7

DIABETIC SMOOTHIES

If you're diabetic, you need to get your doctor's permission before drinking smoothies, because even though they're full of nutrients, some of them are still high in sugar. You're probably a fair hand at picking out the low-glycemic fruits and veggies, but you still need to be careful. Avoid fruits if you can, or at least use only low-glycemic ones, and stick to mostly fiber-rich smoothies rather than juices to avoid insulin spikes.

Now that you understand what to keep away from, let's talk about how beneficial smoothies can be for a diabetic. Especially if you're adding savory smoothies to your diet instead of fruity ones, you're truly doing great things for yourself. Because you're going to drink the smoothie slowly instead of eating it, you're going to reap the benefits of longer, more sustained energy without worrying about insulin spikes.

About 85 percent of diabetics are overweight, and if you're one of them, smoothies may just help you get back on track. Especially if you're a diet-controlled diabetic, you can really benefit from adding a smoothie or two into your daily diet. Get in the habit of having one for breakfast, then another at some other point during the day. They're great as afternoon snacks to tide you over until dinner.

Because they help you feel full and provide a ton of nutrients, you'll most likely find yourself losing weight.

Since weight loss is an essential step on your road back to wellness, smoothies can be a valuable addition to your diet. Read on to find some diabetic-friendly smoothie recipes to get you started.

Taste of Italy

A bit reminiscent of spaghetti sauce, this tastes great and has amazing benefits for your health as well. You're gonna love it!

- 2 tomatoes
- 1 green bell pepper, de-stemmed
- 4 basil leaves
- 2 cloves garlic
- 2 green onions
- 3 oregano leaves

Blend all ingredients together. If you'd like, add some black or cayenne pepper to really snazz it up!

Yield: About 2 cups.

Super Popeye

This smoothie is packed with antioxidants, detoxifiers, and low-glycemic foods that help reverse insulin resistance. Plus the fiber will slow sugar absorption down even further. It tastes green and delicious, but if this flavor is too "green" for you, just add another cucumber or substitute a banana for the artichoke.

- 2 cups spinach
- 1 cup broccoli florets
- 1 artichoke heart
- 1 carrot
- 1 cucumber, quartered

Blend the spinach and broccoli first, then the artichoke, carrot, and cucumber. This is a richly flavored juice and absolutely incredible from a health and diabetic point of view.

Yield: About 3 cups.

Skinny Margarita Smoothie

For those margarita nights with the girls, don't feel left out! You'll find this is a pretty good substitution. If you prefer, feel free to juice it instead of blending.

- 4 celery stalks
- 2 apples, cored and quartered
- 2 limes, peeled
- 1 cup water

Pulse the celery first, and then blend in the apples and the limes. Stir gently and enjoy!

Yield: About 3 cups.

Citrus Serum

This high-fiber, citrus smoothie allows you to get all that juicy, morning flavor you may ordinarily be missing since juice alone may be off the table due to its sugar content. This is low glycemic and packed with healing vitamins.

- 1 orange, peeled
- 1 lemon, peeled
- 1 grapefruit, peeled

Blend all three fruits, and stir. Enjoy.

Yield: About 2 cups.

Slender Sauce

A combination of a low glycemic load, high fiber, and a large quantity of antioxidants and blood sugar stabilizers make this the near-perfect diabetic smoothie. Better still, it's low calorie. It even tastes like a decadent Bloody Mary. The citrus helps prevent oxidation, so feel free to take this one with you for lunch.

- 2 stalks celery
- 1 tomato
- 1 teaspoon horseradish
- 1 lemon wedge, peeled
- 1/4 lime, peeled
- 1/4 teaspoon cayenne pepper

Pulse the celery, tomato, and horseradish. Next, add the lemon, lime, and pepper. Enjoy.

Yield: About 2 cups.

Diabetic Energy Smoothie

The phytonutrients and antioxidants in this smoothie will send your energy levels through the roof without danger of an insulin spike. This one's citrusy and just a bit earthy.

- 1/2 sweet potato
- 1 handful wheatgrass
- 1/2 lemon, peeled
- 1/2 cup cranberries
- 1/2 inch slice ginger
- 1/2 cup water

Cut the sweet potato into 1-inch pieces.

Blend all ingredients together. The lemon protects it from oxidation, so prepare it in the morning, and bring it along to work.

Yield: About 3 cups.

Slow Burn

This yummy twist on traditional, vegetable juice flavor is delicious, and the capsaicin in the pepper gives some extra love to those trying to reverse insulin resistance.

- 1 celery stalk
- 1 tomato
- 1 lemon, peeled
- 2 carrots
- 1/2 jalapeño pepper, de-stemmed

Blend all of your ingredients together. If you can tolerate it, feel free to add more than 1/2 the pepper, as it's one of the main health-promoting ingredients.

Yield: About 2 cups.

The Dish on Celery

The Good: *In addition to all of the great antioxidants and nutrients in celery, it's a great diet food, because it's what's known as a "negative-calorie food." This means when you eat (or drink) celery, your body actually uses more calories digesting it than the celery contains. In other words, you lose weight eating it! Pretty cool, huh?*

The Bad: *There really isn't a downside to celery. It's a great ingredient to lighten up your juice, and the flavor isn't unpleasant.*

Spicy Lemonade

A zesty spin on lemonade, including a surprise kick of jalapeño. The capsaicin in the jalapeño has actually been shown to cure diabetes in mice.

- 3 lemons, peeled
- 1/2 jalapeño pepper, de-stemmed
- 1 cucumber, quartered
- 2 cup water

Blend all ingredients together. As with many of the others, you can take this one to work with you because the citric acid slows down the oxidation.

Yield: About 3 cups.

Slow Down the Sugar Juice

Deliciously green and filling, the apple and cucumber lend a light sweetness that makes this smoothie satisfying. The chlorophyll and flavonoids, along with other nutrients, make this a tasty, low-glycemic meal replacement or snack.

- 1 apple, cored and quartered
- 1/2 cucumber, quartered
- 1/4 lemon, peeled
- 2 kale leaves
- 1 cup spinach
- 1 stalk celery
- 1/4 bulb fennel

Blend all ingredients together.

Yield: About 3 cups.

Gingered Pear

This is a really nice drink that's cool and refreshing. If you'd like to add some cayenne or jalapeño pepper to give it some spice, feel free.

- 1/2 inch slice ginger
- 1 pear, cored and quartered
- 1 apple, cored and quartered
- 1 cucumber, quartered
- 1 stick cinnamon (optional)

Blend all ingredients together and enjoy!

Yield: About 2 cups.

The Dish on Cinnamon

The Good: *Cinnamon is an amazing spice that helps fight wrinkles, promotes clotting, contributes to regulating blood sugar levels, and boosts cognitive function and memory. It's also an antibacterial and tastes delicious!*

The Bad: *Cinnamon has a very distinct flavor that may taste good to you only with very specific foods or other spices.*

8

DIGESTIVE HEALTH SMOOTHIES

Keeping your digestive tract clean is one of the most obvious reasons for drinking smoothies, but there may be a bit more to it than you realize. At any given time, you have up to five pounds of fecal matter and undigested food sitting in your gut that your body has to process and pass. Two of the most important things you can do to keep things running smoothly are eating foods rich in fiber and drinking enough water—drinking smoothies is a great combination of both.

When undigested food sits in your intestines, your body's natural flora and bacteria interact with it and create toxic chemicals and gasses called endotoxins that can damage the lining of your gut. This develops into leaky gut syndrome and allows those toxins to enter your bloodstream. Over time, endotoxins can also upset the delicate balance of good fungi and bacteria in your gut, which consequently may cause problems in your gut, such as increased candida (yeast).

As always, your body will give you hints that there's something wrong, but because the symptoms accrue slowly, you may just write it off as the unavoidable side effects of a busy lifestyle. Some of these symptoms include:

- Brain fog
- Chronic fatigue
- Constipation or diarrhea
- Dull skin
- Joint pain
- Muscle aches
- Skin rashes or acne
- Stomach upset, gas, or bloating

As you can see, some of these symptoms are logically linked to digestive issues, but many of them aren't. The best way to avoid them is to eat a healthful diet. Since life on the run can make it difficult to eat well-balanced, nutrient-dense meals, smoothies you can take with you are a perfect alternative. Try to include foods that are rich in vitamins C, D, and E, because they help keep your digestive tract healthy. Many foods actually help soothe your stomach, too, so these are included in some of the following recipes.

Blended Broccochini Soup

This soup is packed with fiber that will clean out your digestive tract as well as provide all the necessary vitamins to promote optimal health. Cilantro is an antibacterial, is rich in gut-healthful minerals, and also prevents nausea and relieves gas. This smoothie has a rich, spicy flavor you can lighten up, if you like, by adding an apple.

• 1/2 cup water	• 1 cucumber, quartered
• 1 cup broccoli florets	• 1 cup zucchini, cubed
• 2 kale leaves	• 3 small sprigs cilantro

Add the water to the blender first, then add the broccoli and the kale. Pulse until there are only small pieces, then add the rest of the ingredients, and blend until smooth. Serve in a bowl and garnish with a sprig of cilantro.

Yield: About 3 cups.

Peter Rabbit Cocktail Smoothie

Cucumbers are high in both water and fiber, and have been used for years as a natural cure for constipation and stomach upset. The magnesium in the spinach relaxes your intestinal muscles and draws water into your digestive tract. Refreshing and green, the cilantro lends this smoothie a spicy bite.

- 1 carrot
- 2 leaves kale
- 1 small cucumber, quartered
- 1 cup spinach
- 3 small sprigs cilantro
- 1 green apple, cored and quartered
- 1/4 cup water

Blend all ingredients together in the blender. If it's too thick for your taste, add more water, cucumber, or apple.

Yield: About 2 cups.

Cranberry Ginger Julep

Cranberries have anti-adhesion properties that can help prevent ulcers, and ginger and mint have been used as natural digestive aids and anti-nausea treatments for centuries. This light, sweetly spicy drink is a pleasure to drink anytime throughout the day.

- 1 cup cranberries
- 1/2 inch slice ginger
- 1 cucumber, quartered
- 6 mint leaves
- 1/4 cup water

Combine all ingredients in your blender, and pulse until the ingredients are small chunks. Turn up your blender, and puree until it reaches the desired consistency.

Yield: About 2 cups.

Green Sweetie

Strawberries and bananas are great sources of soft fiber that help gently clean your digestive tract while delivering a major nutritional punch. Cabbage is packed with fiber but is best known for its ability to soothe ulcers. This fruity smoothie is delicious, and if you blend it well, you won't even realize the cabbage is there!

- 1 cup cabbage
- 1 banana, peeled
- 1 cup strawberries, capped
- 2 kiwis, peeled
- 1/2 cup water

Add all ingredients to the blender, and puree until extra smooth.

Yield: About 3 cups.

Tropical Soother

Pineapple contains an enzyme called bromelain that helps your body break down and absorb protein, thus improving digestion. It's also full of fiber, as is the plum. The mint and cabbage are also known for helping with digestion, though this smoothie tastes tropical, so very likely you won't notice the presence of the cabbage at all.

- 1/4 pineapple, peeled
- 5 mint leaves
- 1 plum, seeded
- 1/4 head cabbage

Cut the pineapple into 1-inch pieces.

If your pineapple and plum are ripe enough, you may not need water at all, but if you do, add 1/4 cup at a time as you combine the ingredients in the blender. Blend until smooth and enjoy!

Yield: About 2 cups.

> ### The Dish on Pineapples
>
> **The Good:** In addition to all their other health benefits, pineapples contain bromelain, an enzyme that assists digestion by helping to alkalize foods you eat when they reach your stomach. Bromelain also helps regulate digestive secretions from the pancreas and starts breaking down protein so your body can digest it.
>
> **The Bad:** Like most fruits, pineapples are extremely high in sugar, so use them as a healthful component of your breakfast or snack smoothies, but try to include other not-so-sweet ingredients with them.

Reflux Redux

This is alkaline and will help soothe that heartburn. It's also a bit minty, so it won't be bad to sip.

- 1 cup spinach
- 1 carrot with greens
- 1 banana, peeled
- 6 mint leaves

Blend all ingredients together. You may want to add some water to this just to get a good consistency. Also, ginger works really well here, if you'd like to add some.

Yield: About 2 cups.

The Dish on Bananas

The Good: *Bananas act as a natural antacid and are also a great form of gentle fiber. Cool fact: bananas are actually considered a seed, not a fruit. The plant they grow on is, in fact, an herb.*

The Bad: *Bananas don't keep for long, and both refrigeration and brown paper bags hasten the ripening process. To keep you bananas longer, simply store them on the counter in a fruit basket.*

Harvest Helper

Rich in antioxidants as well as flavor, this juice will take you back to the soothing memories of grandma's house in wintertime. It's great for digestion and good health in general.

- 1 sweet potato
- 1 cup pumpkin
- 1 apple, cored and quartered
- 1 teaspoon cinnamon
- 1/2 inch slice ginger
- 1 carrot
- 1/2 cup water

Cut the sweet potato into 1-inch pieces.

Blend all ingredients together.

Yield: About 3 cups.

Slow Gin-ger Fizz

If you have an upset stomach, ginger is one of the best cures. It calms your stomach by relaxing the muscles surrounding it. Sour cherries are a wonderful restorative as well and are excellent for digestion.

- 2 kiwis, peeled
- 1 stalk celery
- 1/2 inch slice ginger
- 1 cucumber, quartered
- 1 apple, cored and quartered
- 1 cup sour cherries, pitted
- 1/2 cup sparkling water

Blend all ingredients together and enjoy.

Yield: About 3 cups.

Feel Beeter Smoothie

Beets and their greens are great for keeping things moving, because they are full of fiber and rich in potassium, iron, beta-carotene, and calcium that your digestive tract needs to stay healthy. The cabbage and apple are great for digestion, as well.

- 3 beets with greens
- 1 apple, cored and quartered
- 1 cup chopped cabbage
- 1 cup water

For this recipe, it's OK to steam the beets a bit to soften them up, though raw is fine, too. Add all ingredients to your blender and blend until smooth.

Yield: About 2 cups.

Honey Ginger Delight

Ginger is great for soothing an upset stomach, and honey provides sweetness and healthful prebiotics. The fruit and yogurt take this belly-soothing smoothie right over the top!

- 1 tablespoon honey
- 1/2 inch slice ginger
- 1 cup plain yogurt
- 1 banana, peeled
- 1 mango, pitted and peeled

Add all ingredients to your blender and blend until smooth.

Yield: About 2 cups.

9

HIGH-ENERGY SMOOTHIES

If you want to get the most out of your body, you have to give it everything it needs to perform at its best. That doesn't mean donuts, energy drinks, pasta, and coffee, either. If you're tired of that 2:00 p.m. collapse or are regularly experiencing brain fog, lethargy, difficulty concentrating, or a general feeling of "blah," then you're probably not getting the nutrients you need to get you through the day. The good news is that as long as you're willing to put down the candy bar and make a few changes to your diet, you'll be running like a track star again in no time at all.

When you continually eat processed foods and simple sugars, two very negative things are taking place that can affect your energy levels. First, you're causing your body to work overtime to eliminate the toxins and indigestible junk you're eating. Second, simple sugars burn quickly and don't provide your body any long-term energy. They've also been linked by research to diseases such as type 2 diabetes, cancer, and possibly even Alzheimer's.

The obvious answer to solving your energy problems and avoiding disease is to minimize your consumption of processed sugars and flours, and to eat more healthful fibers, complex carbohydrates, and plant proteins. This sounds simple, but in reality, it can be tough to take the time to eat balanced meals. Smoothies are the perfect solution for time-sensitive weekdays or action-packed weekends. You'll be healthier, and your energy levels will shoot through the roof, so break out your blender and drink up!

Pineapple Celery Pick-Me-Up

This smoothie is refreshing and great for a little boost of energy to get you through the afternoon. It tastes terrific, too!

- 1/4 pineapple, peeled
- 3 stalks celery
- 1 cucumber, quartered

Cut the pineapple into 1-inch pieces.

Blend all ingredients together and enjoy!

Yield: About 3 cups.

Snap Back Serum

Ginger is an amazing energy booster, and the antioxidants and fiber in this smoothie will keep you going for hours, not to mention preventing that 2:00 p.m. energy crash.

- 1 inch slice ginger
- 1 carrot with greens
- 1 apple, cored and quartered
- 1 lemon, peeled

Blend all ingredients together and enjoy.

Yield: About 2 cups.

The Dish on Apples

The Good: *High in nutrients, fiber, and antioxidants, apples are in fact more effective than a cup of coffee for waking you up in the morning.*

The Bad: *The seeds of apples contain arsenic. Swallowing a seed whole is likely to be fine because your body just passes it through, but don't toss them in the blender, as once they're cracked, the toxin is released.*

Granny's Go Juice

Because it's high in sugar, this one's best as a treat or for breakfast. It's still extremely high in antioxidants, though, along with a long list of health benefits, so don't feel too guilty.

- 1 cup strawberries, capped
- 1 cup blueberries
- 2 carrots
- 1 cup wheatgrass
- 1 beet
- 1 teaspoon cinnamon
- 1/2 cup water

Blend all ingredients together and enjoy!

Yield: About 2 cups.

Belly Soother

In addition to providing a nice energy boost, this smoothie will also help settle your stomach and get you back up and running when you're not feeling your best. It's fresh and citrusy with just a touch of spice.

- 2 sprigs mint
- 1/4 inch slice ginger
- 1 lime, peeled
- 1/2 bulb fennel
- 1 cucumber, quartered
- 1 apple, cored and quartered

Blend all ingredients together. Since it contains lime juice, you can bring it to work without fear of oxidation.

Yield: About 2 cups.

Melon Berry Greenie

Watermelon is one of the best energy boosters on the planet, plus its high water content helps carry its nutrients into your system. This smoothie is both hydrating and delicious!

- 1 cup cranberries
- 2 cups watermelon
- 1 cup spinach

Blend all ingredients together and enjoy.

Yield: About 2 cups.

Greener Goddess Gazpacho

The huge amount of healthful, slow-burning carbs, fiber, antioxidants, vitamins, and minerals, such as iron, in this soup will leave your body clean and your blood oxygenated, while providing you with plenty of sustained energy. The fresh taste will remind you of traditional vegetable juices—but with an extra zing!

- 2 small bunches watercress
- 2 carrots
- 1 tomato
- 5 medium basil leaves
- 1 cup broccoli florets
- 1 green onion
- 1/2 cup water
- Scallions, for garnish

Blend all ingredients in your blender until pureed. If necessary, add more water. Pour into soup bowl, and garnish with scallions. This recipe is tasty as a soup, or you may prefer to water it down a bit and carry with you as a smoothie.

Yield: About 3 cups.

Banana Berry Wake-up Call

Bananas are a great source of vitamin B6, fiber, and slow-burning carbohydrates that help keep your blood sugar steady. The arginine in watermelon helps keep you looking young, while the vitamin C in the pineapple, strawberries, and kiwis in this fruity, refreshing smoothie help keep you going, too!

- 1/4 pineapple, peeled
- 1 cup strawberries, capped
- 1 banana, peeled
- 1 cup watermelon
- 2 kiwis, peeled
- 1/2 cucumber, quartered

Cut the pineapple into 1-inch pieces.

Toss ingredients into the blender a few at a time and puree.

Yield: About 4 cups.

Green Island Goodness

There are only four ingredients in this tropical-tasting smoothie, but the nutrients it contains are out of this world! Arugula delivers energy-sustaining protein as well as the B complex vitamins that your body uses both for short-term and long-term energy production. The potassium in the banana and the high-fiber content of the entire smoothie keep your blood sugar stable, allowing you to sail through your day.

- 1/4 pineapple, peeled
- 2 cups arugula
- 1 banana, peeled
- 1/2 cup water

Cut the pineapple into 1-inch pieces.

Add all ingredients to your blender and puree. The color of this one is a fun, bright green—enjoy!

Yield: About 2 cups.

Zesty Garden Greenie

Rich in biotin, thiamin, vitamin C, and even iron, this zesty, salad-flavored smoothie will provide steady energy throughout your day, while fighting disease and brain fog. It's truly a glass of goodness with a taste reminiscent of a fresh, Italian tomato sauce.

- 1/2 cup water
- 2 carrots
- 1 tomato
- 2 cloves garlic
- 3 kale leaves
- 1/2 lemon, peeled

Add water and carrots to your blender, and pulse a few times to chunk the carrots. Add the rest of the ingredients, and puree until it reaches the desired consistency. Enjoy!

Yield: About 3 1/2–4 cups.

Tropical Blast Booster

The combination of B vitamins, minerals, iron, quality carbohydrates, and fiber in this smoothie makes it a great, afternoon pick-me-up. It's also excellent for breakfast, and you probably won't even taste the spinach over the fruity, tropical berry flavors.

- 1/4 pineapple, peeled
- Seeds from 1 pomegranate
- 1 cup blueberries
- 2 cups spinach

Cut the pineapple into 1-inch pieces.

Add all ingredients to your blender and puree. If you'd like it a bit thinner, just add water, but its chewy deliciousness just as it is makes it extremely satisfying.

Yield: About 2 cups.

The Dish on Spinach

The Good: *Packed with fiber, complex carbohydrates, B vitamins, and twelve other vitamins, spinach truly is a nutritional powerhouse. It's loaded with vitamin C that supports your adrenal glands, and can therefore reduce stress and fatigue.*

The Bad: *Spinach is high in oxalates that can contribute to kidney and gall stones if eaten in large amounts regularly, so switch up your leafy greens!*

10

GREEN SMOOTHIE RECIPES

You've probably seen other people drinking them—glasses of what appear to be pureed yard clippings. Before you turn your nose up at the idea, let's get a few things straight. To begin with, the only reason it's called a green smoothie is because something in it makes it green. That doesn't necessarily mean spinach: remember that delicious produce such as apples, grapes, kiwi, and cucumbers are green as well. You can use other fruits and vegetables, too. A smoothie made from kiwi, cucumbers, bananas, and oranges is still a green smoothie—just look at the color!

Throughout the pages of this book, you've learned about all kinds of ways that smoothies are good for you, but green smoothies really take it to the next nutritional level. The element that makes them green is in fact at the heart of what makes them so beneficial for your health: chlorophyll. This is the green pigment responsible for signaling photosynthesis, the process that uses light to convert water and carbon dioxide into glucose, the plant's energy source.

The reason many professionals think chlorophyll is so good for humans is because it's nearly identical to hemoglobin, the part of your blood that transports oxygen. It hasn't yet been proven that

chlorophyll provides the same functions as hemoglobin, but prelimi-
nary research strongly suggests it. Chlorophyll offers several other
health benefits as well, including:

- Acting as an antioxidant to protect you from free radical damage
- Boosting your body's healing abilities
- Improving your skin tone
- Increasing alkalinity
- Preventing brain fog
- Providing steady levels of energy
- Removing heavy metals from your blood
- Stabilizing blood sugar
- Supporting weight loss

The thing about chlorophyll is that it's damaged or even destroyed
by the cooking process. Once the produce loses that bright green color
and turns olive, you've already lost all of chlorophyll's health benefits,
so drinking smoothies is a perfect way to ensure you're getting all
of the good things your greens have to offer!

Kale Cocktail

*Talk about a glass of nutrition! This smoothie is bursting with chlorophyll
as well as vitamins A, C, E, and K. The varied supply of antioxidants will
help fight disease, and the green flavor and generous quantity of fiber will
keep you full for hours. If it tastes too "green," just add a cucumber.*

• 6 kale leaves	• 1 green bell pepper, de-stemmed
• 1 cup spinach	
• 1 cup collard greens	• 1 clove garlic
	• 1 cup water

Blend all ingredients together. If you'd like, add a pinch of sea salt
or black pepper to really bring out the individual flavors.

Yield: About 2 cups.

Cucumber Carrot Cocktail

Don't let the bizarre color of this one fool you; it's refreshing and delicious. It's also packed with vitamins A and C, as well as chlorophyll and a whole host of other goodies.

- 1 cucumber, quartered
- 1 carrot with greens

- 1 apple, cored and quartered
- 1 lemon, peeled

Blend all ingredients. This one is OK to take with you for lunch, because the lemon juice helps prevent oxidation from taking place.

Yield: About 2 cups.

Broccolichoke Juice

If you're the average person, the name might put you off, but give it a shot. The garlic adds an Italian flavor and blends well with the other ingredients to provide a nutritional powerhouse of a smoothie. If the flavor is too strong, just add another cucumber or a banana.

- 1 cup broccoli florets
- 1 artichoke heart
- 1 carrot with greens

- 1 clove garlic
- 1 small cucumber, quartered

Blend all ingredients together. You should probably add 1 cup water with this recipe unless you like it really thick.

Yield: About 2 cups.

Green Beast

This is a nice, smoothly textured smoothie that's outstanding for digestion and disease prevention. It tastes fairly light and just a bit fruity.

- 1 cup spinach
- 1 banana, peeled
- 3 stalks celery
- 1 cucumber, quartered
- 1 carrot

Blend all ingredients together. This juice packs a nutritional punch you won't find in many other combinations, yet still tastes really good. If you want to spice it up a bit, throw in some black or cayenne pepper after you've poured it in the glass.

Yield: About 2 cups.

Pepper Zing

This is a pleasantly refreshing juice that has a wonderfully saucy taste. It's great for lunch because it offers a nice, nutritional boost without feeling heavy.

- 2 green bell peppers, de-stemmed
- 1 tomato
- 4 stalks celery
- 2 basil leaves
- 1/2 jalapeño pepper, de-stemmed (optional)

Blend all ingredients together and enjoy.

Yield: About 2 cups.

A Is for Apple Smoothie

This smoothie is filling and refreshing. The sweet taste makes it delicious for breakfast or a snack, and the ginger offers a hint of spice and sophistication. It's also full of vitamin C and antioxidants.

- 1 green apple, cored and quartered
- 1 cucumber, quartered
- 1 cup grapes
- 1/2 inch slice ginger

Blend it all up and enjoy!

Yield: About 2 cups.

Green Shield

Rich in chlorophyll and vitamin C, this smoothie has a fresh green flavor with a bit of spice. If you'd like to lower the heat, simply remove the seeds from the pepper.

- 2 stalks celery
- 1 green bell peppers, de-stemmed
- 4 asparagus tips
- 1 lemon, peeled
- 1 jalapeño pepper, de-stemmed (optional)

Just as you do when you cook it, break your asparagus at the natural break. If you want to spice your smoothie up and gain the benefits of capsaicin, throw a jalapeño into the blender or some cayenne.

Yield: About 3 cups.

The Dish on Jalapeños

The Good: *The capsaicin in peppers is an amazing disease fighter and helps protect you from everything from the common cold to cancer. Its anti-inflammatory properties help with arthritis and heart health. It also kicks your metabolism into high gear!*

The Bad: *Though flavorful and good for you, jalapeños can be brutally hot, so you may want to use rubber gloves when handling them. A useful fact: you can reduce the heat by taking out the seeds.*

Fruit Greenie

Refreshing, delicious, and full of antioxidants, this smoothie will be one of your favorites if you like a drink that's light and mildly fruity. It's easy to make, so grab it on your way out the door instead of skipping meals!

- 2 kiwis, peeled
- 1 small bunch wheatgrass
- 4 medium strawberries, capped
- 1/2 cucumber, quartered

Blend all ingredients and drink immediately. If you want a drink that you can take for lunch, toss in 1/2 lemon to help avoid oxidation. These flavors pair well here.

Yield: About 2 cups.

Kidney Cleansing Juice

Dandelion greens appear once again because they're excellent for your kidneys. The lemon juice is also advantageous if you have calcium stones. This green smoothie has a nice, clean flavor, thanks to the basil and lemon.

- 5 celery stalks
- 6 basil leaves
- 1 lemon, peeled
- 2 kale leaves
- 1 tomato

Blend all ingredients together.

Yield: About 3 cups.

Snooze Juice

If you want to sleep, the number-one fruit to eat is the cherry, due to its melatonin content. This recipe contains melatonin and other nutrients known to reduce anxiety and induce sleep. The ginger will soothe your belly, too.

- 1/2 cup cherries, frozen
- 1 pear, cored and quartered
- 1 apple, cored and quartered
- 1/2 zucchini
- 1/2 inch slice ginger
- 1 carrot
- 1 cup spinach
- 1/2 cup water

Blend everything together and enjoy—this juice actually tastes quite delicious.

Yield: About 3 cups.

11

HEALTHFUL SKIN RECIPES

Has your skin gone from looking dewy and fresh to gray and blotchy? Maybe you constantly fight breakouts of acne or are starting to notice age spots and discolorations caused by the sun and years of exposure to environmental toxins. Regardless of your skin issue, chances are pretty good that it can be improved by drinking enough water and eating plenty of fruits and vegetables.

Your body has only three means of ridding itself of toxins: your digestive tract, your respiratory system, and your skin. It stands to reason, then, that if you aren't healthy on the inside, you're not going to *look* healthy on the outside.

If you're constantly overloading your system with processed junk, it's no wonder you have complexion problems. To compound the problem, there are toxins in your foods, in the things you touch, and even in the air you breathe that create tissue-damaging, disease-causing free radicals. Because you're constantly exposed, it's vital that you give your body what it needs to fight those free radicals if you want to remain healthy inside and out.

Though you can improve your complexion by simply replacing your junk food habit with healthful fruits and vegetables, there are some specific nutrients that can really give your skin a boost. Look for collagen-boosting vitamin C and magnesium, as well as the super antioxidant and restorative vitamin A. B vitamins help your skin rejuvenate, omega-3 fatty acids are also extremely beneficial, and fiber helps keep your digestive tract healthy, which contributes to healthy skin as well.

Generally speaking, a smoothie is the perfect way to get several servings of skin-healthful nutrients on the run! Here are some great recipes to get you started.

Potato Head

Potatoes are often used as an alternative treatment for acne, and the vitamin A in tomatoes really helps your skin to glow.

- 2 potatoes
- 6 basil leaves

- 1 tomato

Cut the potatoes into 1-inch pieces.

Blend all ingredients together and enjoy. Feel free to throw some parsley in, too, if you'd like.

Yield: About 2 cups.

The Dish on Potatoes

The Good: *Potatoes are alkalizing and therefore help balance your pH. High acidity is associated with acne, so potatoes are often used in natural acne cleanses.*

The Bad: *Potatoes are extremely high in starch, which converts straight to glucose. Use with care, especially if you're diabetic.*

Green with Envy

Adding this drink to your juicing schedule a couple of times per week will have everyone green with envy over your stunning complexion!

- 1 cup broccoli florets
- 1 cucumber, quartered
- 1 kale leaf
- 1 green bell pepper, de-stemmed
- 1 tomato
- 1 celery stalk
- 1 cup water

Blend all ingredients together. The chlorophyll, antioxidants, and vitamins A and C in these vegetables will have your skin glowing in no time.

Yield: About 3 cups.

See Your Way to Beauty

This juice combines produce that's rich in vitamins A and C. It's great for both your skin and eyes, and fights disease and aging, too. The lemongrass and arugula add zing in addition to a huge nutritional boost. Its flavor is refreshing, earthy, and a bit peppery.

- 1/2 sweet potato
- 1 cucumber, quartered
- 1 carrot with greens
- 1 cup arugula
- 1/4 pound lemongrass

Cut the sweet potato into 1-inch pieces.

Blend all ingredients together well. The leafy greens combined with the beta-carotene in the carrots and sweet potatoes really give this juice a boost that will make your skin radiant and your eyes dazzling. Plus it tastes delicious, too. Feel free to toss in some cinnamon, if you like, for an additional kick of nutrition and flavor!

Yield: About 3 cups.

Passionberry Orange

Passion fruit and orange juice contain large amounts of vitamins A and C, while berries add antioxidant power that stops the free radicals that cause wrinkles. Look younger and more radiant by adding this juice into your smoothie for breakfast or a pick-me-up.

- 1 orange, peeled
- 1 cup passion fruit
- 1 cup mixed berries
- 1 carrot with greens

Blend ingredients together well and drink immediately, because the delicate nutrients in this particular smoothie will start to deteriorate quickly.

Yield: About 3 cups.

The Dish on Carrots

The Good: *In addition to boosting eye health and preventing disease, carrots are great for your cleansing smoothies because the fiber helps clean out your digestive tract, and vitamin A (beta-carotene) is essential for proper liver function.*

The Bad: *The beta-carotene in carrots and other produce can actually affect the color or your skin. Though this side effect is thought to be harmless, you may want to avoid eating an entire basket of carrots at a time unless you are fond of that orange hue. As with everything, moderation is the key!*

Green Vichyssoise

Potatoes are alkalizing and help to balance the pH of your skin, which is one cause of acne. The sulfur and antioxidants in the onions and garlic are helpful in that respect as well. This tastes like a traditional potato soup, so feel free to enjoy it in a bowl for lunch or dinner.

- 2 red potatoes
- 1/4 red onion
- 2 cloves garlic
- 3 sprigs parsley
- 2 cups spinach
- 1 teaspoon rosemary
- 1 teaspoon thyme
- 1 cup water

Cut the red potatoes into 1-inch pieces.

Add all the ingredients to your blender and puree. Serve in a bowl and garnish with a parsley and rosemary sprig.

Yield: About 4 cups.

Mediterranean Beauty Blend

Zucchini is one of those undervalued foods that is incredibly good for you. One of its benefits is that it contains proline, an amino acid that promotes collagen synthesis. This fresh-tasting, earthy smoothie is great as a soup as well, so enjoy it however you'd like!

- 1/2 cup water
- 1 zucchini
- 1 cucumber, quartered
- 1 green bell pepper, de-stemmed
- 2 sprigs dill
- 2 springs parsley, plus extra for garnish

Add water, zucchini, and cucumber to your blender and pulse. Add the pepper and herbs, and puree. Serve in a bowl and garnish with parsley, or pour it in a glass for a hearty meal on the go.

Yield: About 3 cups.

Summer Garden Smoothie

Everyone knows that broccoli and tomatoes are chock full of nutrients, but arugula has three grams of protein per serving, as well as potassium, magnesium, iron, zinc, folate, B6, and vitamins A and C—all important nutrients your skin needs to be healthy. You can't go wrong with this smoothie, no matter what's ailing you, and fresh veggie flavor will take you back to the delicious gardens of your childhood!

- 1/2 cup water
- 1 cup broccoli florets
- 1 tomato

- 2 sprigs parsley
- 1 cucumber, quartered
- 2 cups arugula

Combine the water and broccoli in the blender, and pulse until the broccoli is chunked. Add the rest of the ingredients and puree.

Yield: About 4 cups.

Hidden Beauty Smoothie

This is a simple, tropical-tasting drink, but don't let the lack of ingredients fool you. The three it contains are packed with potassium, vitamins A and C, and dietary fiber, which help keep your skin clear and soft.

- 1/4 pineapple, peeled
- 2 cups spinach

- 1 banana, peeled

Cut the pineapple into 1-inch pieces.

Add all ingredients to your blender, and puree until the smoothie reaches the texture you desire.

Yield: About 2 cups.

Doctor Away Puree

Packed with vitamins, antioxidants, and amino acids, this smoothie will help keep your system clean while skin cells rejuvenate to give you a bright, clear complexion. Its lightly fruity, green flavor is pleasant to drink without tasting cloyingly sweet or overly green.

- 1 green apple, cored and quartered
- 2 kiwis, peeled
- 2 cups romaine lettuce, chopped
- 2 springs parsley
- 1/2 cup water

Add all ingredients to your blender and puree. Pour into a glass and enjoy!

Yield: About 2 cups.

12

KID-FRIENDLY SMOOTHIES

G etting kids to eat healthfully is sometimes an uphill battle, especially with a fast-food restaurant on every corner and grocery stores full of junk food. Combine that with the time restraints of being a working parent, and it's nearly enough to make you throw your hands up in despair. But don't give up just yet. On the pages to come are plenty of recipes for quick, healthful smoothies that your kids will love. They'll never know they're good for them unless you spill the...er...broccoli!

Before getting into the recipes, however, let's take a look at some of the nutrients your kids need most to keep them healthy and help them grow both physically and cognitively.

Omega-3 fatty acids are essential for proper brain development, while complex carbohydrates provide steady energy and work with fiber to help keep blood sugar levels stable. Kids need protein to help them build muscle, and calcium to promote healthful bone growth. Vitamins A and C are necessary for healthy skin and healing, too—leafy greens and citrus fruits are great sources of these antioxidant vitamins.

Everyone knows that what kids need and what they are willing to eat are often two vastly different things. Since it's always better to get nutrition from natural food sources rather than supplements, feel free to toss in anything you'd like to see if your kids will drink it. You'll be amazed how much spinach you can get in a glass when you also add bananas, strawberries, pineapple, or other delicious, kid-friendly fruits as camouflage.

The plus side is that many kids will actually *like* the look of a green smoothie, so let's get started—you're going to be surprised at how easy this actually is!

Apriloupe Delight

The vitamins and minerals in this smoothie are outstanding for muscle growth and cognitive function. They'll be getting two servings of veggies, and if you don't tell them, they won't even know it!

- 1 cup cantaloupe, peeled and seeded
- 1 carrot, with or without the greens
- 2 apricots, pitted
- 1/2 cup broccoli florets

Blend everything together, and watch them slurp it down.

Yield: About 2 cups.

Pineapple Cherry Yummy

This pretty, pink smoothie will be a favorite with the kids, and the health benefits of the cherries and beets just can't be overstated.

- 1/4 pineapple, peeled
- 2 plums, seeded
- 1 cup sour cherries, pitted
- 1/2 beet
- 1/2 cup cow's milk or almond milk

Cut the pineapple into 1-inch pieces.

Blend everything together, and smile while they drink down their fruits and veggies.

Yield: About 3 cups.

Green Apple Grape

This one is packed with vitamin C and brain-boosting vitamin E and omega-3s. Its smooth texture and familiar flavors will no doubt have them begging for another glass.

- 1 cup honeydew, peeled and seeded
- 1 cup red grapes
- 1 green apple, cored and quartered
- 1 avocado, pitted and peeled

Blend it all up and enjoy. Just don't forget to share with the kids!

Yield: About 3 cups.

The Dish on Grapes

The Good: *Green grapes are an excellent source of chlorophyll, while red ones are rich in disease-fighting polyphenols. Grapes have also been shown to improve memory and math scores, and are high in water, fiber, antioxidants, vitamins, and trace minerals that help kids grow and stay healthy.*

The Bad: *Unlike many other fruits, grapes won't get any riper once they are picked, so be sure to purchase the ripest grapes when shopping.*

Popeye's Fruit Smoothie

Tricky mommy, hiding that spinach in a glass of yumminess! In addition to healthful vitamins A and C, the spinach and milk are both excellent sources of calcium.

- 1 cup frozen strawberries, capped
- 1 cup raspberries or blueberries
- 1 banana, peeled
- 1 cup spinach
- 1 cup cow's milk or almond milk

Blend all ingredients together and enjoy.

Yield: About 3 cups.

Hopping Banana Smoothie

The color's a bit odd, so you may want to put this in a sippy cup, or drink a glass yourself so they'll want to try it, too. This smoothie is packed with potassium and antioxidants as well as beta-carotene that helps with brain function and eyesight.

- 1 banana, peeled
- 1 apple, cored and quartered, or 1/2 cup organic apple juice
- 1 carrot with greens
- 1 cup plain or vanilla yogurt

Blend all ingredients together, and watch them enjoy.

Yield: About 2 cups.

Green Goblin

They will love drinking this as much as you will love watching them slurp down all that heart- and brain-healthful goodness.

- 1 banana, peeled
- 1 cup green grapes
- 1 apple, cored and quartered
- 1 cup vanilla yogurt
- 1/2 cup fresh broccoli florets

Blend all ingredients well.

Yield: About 2 cups.

The Green Peach

This is another green smoothie that your kids will love. Packed with vitamins A and C, several B vitamins, and potassium, this one's as good for them as it tastes.

- 5 fresh strawberries, capped
- 1 peach, pitted
- 1 cup spinach
- 1/2 cup organic orange juice
- 1/2 cup almond milk
- 1 cup ice

Blend together all ingredients until smooth.

Yield: About 2 cups.

Strawberry Go-Getter

This smoothie has healthful carbs and B vitamins that provide quick energy combined with enough fiber content to keep kids going for hours. It's a lightly fruity and delicious treat!

- 10 fresh strawberries, capped
- 1 banana, peeled
- 1/2 cup broccoli florets
- 1/2 cup apple juice
- 1/2 cup blueberries
- 1/2 cup plain or vanilla Greek yogurt

Blend all ingredients together. If you prefer, add some ice and make it a shake!

Yield: About 2 cups.

Berry Yummy Smoothie

The tasty, berry flavor and funky green color will make this a hit with your kids. In addition to all of the vitamins and antioxidants they gain from the fruit, they're also getting a nice kick of chlorophyll, vitamin C, and minerals from the veggies, too.

- 1 cup raspberries
- 1 cup strawberries, capped
- 1/2 cup peas
- 1/2 cup spinach
- 1 cup vanilla yogurt
- 1/2 cow's milk or almond milk

Blend ingredients well and enjoy. As with the others, if you'd like to drink it frozen, just add ice!

Yield: About 2 1/2 cups.

The Dish on Peas

The Good: *Peas are a first-rate source of vitamins A, B6, and C. They're also rich in magnesium, potassium, and iron, and are naturally full of fiber.*

The Bad: *The only round, green food that many kids will eat is M&M'S, and there's no way you can pass a pea off as that! Toss them in a smoothie, and they'll never know.*

Beach Vacation

The tropical flavors of this smoothie will have them begging for a refill and a trip to the beach, even in the middle of the winter. It's a great source of vitamins A, B6, and C, magnesium, niacin, and betalain to keep them growing and developing to their full potential!

- 1/4 pineapple, peeled
- 1 avocado, pitted and peeled
- 1 cup mango, pitted and peeled
- 1 banana, peeled
- 1/2 cup apple juice or pineapple juice

Cut the pineapple into 1-inch pieces.

Blend it all up, and watch it disappear. You may want to make enough for two!

Yield: About 2 cups.

13

LOW-FAT SMOOTHIES

If you're looking for some great recipes to help you burn fat and get skinny, this chapter has just the ones for you. Though nearly all fruits and vegetables are fat-free or have only healthful fats, some vegetables are particularly low in the bad stuff contributing to that spare tire, which constantly attempts to settle around your waist.

Since many people make smoothies with milk or yogurt to boost flavor and protein levels, this is where you need to pay special attention. Since all-fruit or veggie-only smoothies are fat-free, this chapter is going to concentrate specifically on smoothies that contain other ingredients, so you can learn what non-produce ingredients are good to use as part of a low-fat diet.

The first ingredient that adds a ton of fat is full-fat yogurt. Instead, try low-fat Greek yogurt. It will add a nice protein boost and will lend an extremely rich, creamy texture to your smoothies. If you just like to add a splash or two of milk, try switching from full-fat, whole cow's milk to skim milk. Original or vanilla almond milk is another great alternative: it's lower in fat, higher in protein, and lends a mildly nutty flavor. Finally, if you insist on adding protein powder to your smoothie, make sure that it's low fat or fat-free.

Veggie Delite

This recipe contains no fat at all and is packed with phytonutrients, heart-healthful chlorophyll, and even capsaicin, that sugar-regulating superstar. The yummy, veggie flavor is like vegetable juice, but all pumped up!

- 1 tomato
- 4 basil leaves
- 1 carrot
- 1 bell pepper, de-stemmed

- 1/2 cup water
- 1 teaspoon horseradish
- 1/4 teaspoon cayenne
- 1 pinch sea salt and cracked black pepper (optional)

Blend all ingredients together and enjoy!

Yield: About 2 cups.

The Dish on Full-Spectrum, Unprocessed Sea Salt

The Good: *Salt has been demonized over the past few decades, but the truth of the matter is that your body needs a certain amount of sodium. Not processed white table salt—only natural sea salt. Sea salt offers sodium as well as many other trace minerals that your body requires to function properly. Used in moderation, sea salt is beneficial for most people and adds flavor to savory smoothies.*

The Bad: *If you have high blood pressure, kidney problems, or other health issues, make sure that you consult your doctor before you add salt to your diet.*

Recovery Tonic

Rich in potassium, calcium, and antioxidants, this smoothie even contains protein and omega-3s, so it makes a super recovery drink after you work out!

- 1 red potato
- 1 cucumber, quartered
- 1 stalk celery
- 1 cup spinach
- 1 yellow squash
- 1 cup broccoli florets

Cut the red potato into 1-inch pieces.

Blend all ingredients and enjoy.

Yield: About 3 cups.

Green Beet Smoothie

Rich in vitamins A, C, E, and K, this smoothie is fantastic if you're trying to add nutrients without loading up on calories and fat.

- 1 carrot with greens
- 1 yellow beet
- 2 celery stalks
- 1 cucumber, quartered
- 1 green bell pepper, de-stemmed

Blend all ingredients together and drink immediately.

Yield: About 3 cups.

Veggie Vitae

Another nutritionally dense, fat-free smoothie, this one has a lighter flavor and makes a great afternoon refresher.

- 1 cup spinach
- 1 small cucumber, quartered
- 2 stalks celery
- 3 carrots with greens
- 1/2 apple, cored and quartered
- 1/2 cup water or apple juice

Blend all ingredients and enjoy.

Yield: About 3 cups.

Beet Juice Supreme

Not everyone appreciates the exceptional, nutritional value of beets, and if you don't, you're really missing out! The betalain plays a key role in cellular detoxification, and the antioxidants fight all kinds of diseases. This brightly colored, veggie-flavored juice has a subtle sweetness you'll find delightful!

- 1 beet
- 1 tomato
- 2 stalks celery
- 1 cucumber, quartered

Blend all ingredients together. Add 1/2 cup water if you need a bit more liquid.

Yield: About 2 cups.

The Dish on Tomatoes

The Good: *Tomatoes contain benefits for everything from eye health to weight loss—and are even a negative-calorie food. They boast one of the highest nutritional values of any fruit.*

The Bad: *Because tomatoes are a negative-calorie food, be sure that when you're using them as a base for your weight-loss juices, you incorporate enough calories to keep you healthy.*

Seriously Green

This easy, bare-bones green smoothie is pure nutrition in a glass. Though it may sound really "green," you'll be surprised at how light its flavor actually is. The boost of chlorophyll and vitamins A, B5, C, and niacin make this a disease-fighting, fat-blasting machine!

- 2 stalks celery
- 1 cucumber, quartered
- 2 cups spinach
- 1 apple, cored and quartered
- 1 cup water

Blend all ingredients together and enjoy!

Yield: About 2 cups.

Fennel and Greens

You may want to add an apple or tomato to bring the flavors here back to familiar territory, but it's delicious just the way it is. This smoothie is highly beneficial for your digestive and immune systems, and gives your brain a nice boost, too.

- 2 carrots with greens
- 2 cups spinach
- 1/4 bulb fennel with greens
- 2 lemon wedges, peeled
- 1 cucumber, quartered
- 1/2 teaspoon cayenne

Blend all ingredients well. Typically found in many Italian dishes, fennel lends a nice, peppery flavor to your smoothie.

Yield: About 3 cups.

Green Magic

This book hasn't done much with Brussels sprouts, but you should use them as much as possible if you're trying to shed some pounds. They're packed with all the nutrients greens normally contain, plus a ton of fiber and an appetizing crunch.

- 3 stalks celery
- 6 oregano leaves
- 2 cups spinach
- 1 cucumber, quartered
- 1 tomato
- 6 Brussels sprouts

Blend all ingredients together.

Yield: About 3 cups.

Strawberry Tomato Smoothie

It sounds odd but is actually delicious! These flavors meld together for a blast of flavorful freshness, while delivering a glass full of carotenoids and flavonoids that protect your cells from damage.

- 6 strawberries, capped
- 1 tomato
- 3 carrots
- 2 stalks celery
- 1/2 cup water

Blend all ingredients well. There is some citric acid in the strawberries, so you may be OK storing this one until lunch.

Yield: About 2 cups.

Spicy Cabbage Stew

This is a smoothie version of that delicious cabbage stew your grandma used to make. It's rich in chlorophyll and minerals, and even offers the diabetes-fighting, fat-burning capsaicin in the pepper.

- 2 green bell peppers, de-stemmed
- 3 green onions with stalks
- 1/4 head cabbage
- 1/2 jalapeño pepper, de-stemmed
- 2 stalks celery
- 2 carrots
- 1/2 cup water or tomato juice

Blend all ingredients well and drink immediately.

Yield: About 3 cups.

14

PROTEIN SMOOTHIES

Drinking a post-workout smoothie is a great way to obtain the protein your body needs to recover properly. It helps you build the tissues you just shredded and will also help prevent muscle soreness. You need to make sure it's quality protein, though; otherwise you're either wasting your time or actually doing harm to your body. Therefore, let's discuss the differences between proteins so that you can make an informed decision.

- **Plant Protein:** Though plant proteins don't generally offer all the amino acids you need, there are several benefits to including these in your diet. Plant proteins don't contain unhealthful fats like many sources of animal proteins do, and they offer protection against chronic degenerative diseases and cardiovascular disease.

- **Soy Protein:** Extracted from the soybean, soy protein is a complete protein but also contains controversial phytoestrogens that bond to estrogen receptors in the body. If you choose to use soy protein, go for the soy isolate rather than the soy concentrate, because it's a much purer form of protein.

- **Whey Protein:** Whey is a dairy-based product that's rich in essential amino acids. As a matter of fact, it's a complete protein, which means that it contains every amino acid your body needs. It's the most bioavailable source of protein, which means that it's the easiest for your body to use. Regardless of whether you choose to add some protein powder to your breakfast smoothie, your post-workout smoothie, or your meal-replacement smoothie, make sure that you're using a high-quality protein. Just like when you're choosing your produce, now is not the time to sacrifice health for economy. High-protein produce includes seaweed and spirulina. Artichokes, leafy greens, apples, cantaloupes, and beets also contain small amounts of protein. Finally, almond milk and yogurt are excellent, natural sources of protein.

The Dish on Soy

The Good: *Soy is a great source of complete protein, isoflavones, and fiber, all of which have numerous health benefits.*

The Bad: *Some research suggests that soy may inhibit iron uptake, so if you tend to be anemic, you may want to opt for another source. Also, since the phytoestrogens in soy may act the same as human estrogen, many men avoid it as well. For the sake of simplicity, this book will use whey protein in these smoothies, but feel free to do your own research and choose as you see fit.*

Chocolate Nut

This is a first-rate, post-workout or breakfast smoothie. It packs a protein wallop as well as functional complex carbs and omega-3s that will help you recover and keep you running for hours.

- 1 scoop chocolate whey protein
- 1 banana, peeled

- 1/2 cup rolled oats
- 2 tablespoons almond butter
- 1 cup water or coconut water

Blend all ingredients together and enjoy!

Yield: About 2 cups.

The Dish on Almond Butter

The Good: *Almond butter adds a delicious, nutty flavor to your smoothies and is packed with antioxidants, helps keep your cholesterol and blood sugars regulated, and delivers a huge protein punch. It's also full of fiber so it helps you feel fuller longer.*

The Bad: *Almond butter doesn't come cheap, and though it's incredibly healthful, it's high in calories, so try to use it in moderation.*

Plum Protein

Packed with protein, potassium, magnesium, and cell-protecting, disease-fighting flavonoids, this smoothie is an excellent choice anytime. It's also rich in fiber, so you'll stay full for hours.

- 1 scoop vanilla whey protein
- 1 plum, pitted
- 1 banana, peeled
- 1 cup water
- 1/2 cup ice cubes

Blend all ingredients and enjoy!

Yield: About 3 cups.

Pomegranate Cherry Smoothie

This one is packed with tasty, natural plant proteins. Though there are obviously less than if you'd added a scoop of protein powder, you still get heaps of nutrients, including vitamins A, B complex, and C, as well as chlorophyll. Not to mention pomegranates and cherries may actually prevent some forms of cancer.

- 1 cup pomegranate seeds
- 1/2 cup sour cherries, pitted
- 2 kiwis, peeled
- 1/2 cup blackberries
- 2 beets
- 1/2 cup water

Blend all ingredients well and enjoy.

Yield: About 3 cups.

Muscle Ache Drink

Greens are packed with minerals that help your muscles recover from tough workouts. You'll be surprised here how little you actually taste the greens.

- 1 cup broccoli florets
- 1 cup spinach
- 1 apple, cored and quartered
- 6 kale leaves
- 1 banana, peeled

Blend all ingredients well.

Yield: About 3 cups.

Ginger Apple Fizz

Ginger is exceptional for digestion, and the complex carbs and fiber will give you sustained energy.

- 1/2 inch slice ginger
- 2 apples, cored and quartered
- 1 pear, cored and quartered
- 1 scoop whey protein
- 1 cup sparkling water

Blend all ingredients and enjoy!

Yield: About 2 cups.

Citri-Berry Chiller

The vitamin C in this smoothie will keep you healthy, while the protein in the almond milk will help you recover from any ailments. If you like, throw in some ice to make it a fruity shake!

- 1/4 pineapple, peeled
- 1/2 cup orange juice
- 4 medium strawberries, capped
- 1/2 cup almond milk

Cut the pineapple into 1-inch pieces.

Blend all ingredients and enjoy!

Yield: About 3 cups.

Seeing Green

Rich in vitamin C, potassium, calcium, and about twenty other nutrients, this is a top-notch protein drink that will help keep both your muscles and brain functioning properly. It tastes fruity and delicious, too!

- 1 cup spinach
- 2 apples, cored and quartered
- 1 cucumber, quartered
- 1 banana, peeled
- 1 scoop fat-free plain or vanilla Greek yogurt

Blend all ingredients and drink immediately!

Yield: About 3 cups.

Green Energy

The fiber and chlorophyll in this smoothie will give you an energy burst that will last for hours. The leafy greens also provide plenty of veggie protein, so blend away.

- 2 cups spinach
- 1 bunch wheatgrass
- 2 cups broccoli florets
- 1 cucumber, quartered
- 1 banana, peeled

Blend all ingredients together and enjoy.

Yield: About 2 cups.

C to See Juice

Rich in carotenoids, disease-fighting lutein, and vitamin C, this protein smoothie tastes pumpkiny, earthy, and sweet.

- 2 sweet potatoes
- 2 carrots
- 1 cup cantaloupe, peeled and seeded
- 1 cup fat-free vanilla Greek yogurt

Cut the sweet potatoes into 1-inch pieces.

Blend ingredients together, adding ice and a splash of milk if you'd like to drink it frozen.

Yield: About 3 cups.

Simply Orangalicious!

It's incredibly simple, but you're going to love this one. The almond milk adds a bit of an exotic flavor as well as a healthful amount of protein.

- 1 orange, peeled
- 1 banana, peeled

- 1/2 cup almond milk

Blend all ingredients together, and add ice if you'd like.

Yield: About 3 cups.

15

WEIGHT-LOSS SMOOTHIES

When it comes to losing weight, one of the biggest challenges you may face is hunger. The simple fact of the matter is that to lose weight, you have to decrease calories and fat. That often means eating significantly less than you may be accustomed to. The secret is to find foods low in calories and bad fats, yet high in filling ingredients such as fiber to stave off feelings of hunger for several hours. It's important to have a sustained source of energy as well, because research shows that when people feel tired, they often head to the fridge.

Though all produce is low in calories and generally fat-free, not all are created equal. When your goal is to lose weight, you need to have foods that taste great, keep you full, provide the nutrition you need, and give you the necessary energy to get through the day: this equates to fiber and complex carbs. For your breakfast smoothies, try going a bit sweeter to use that natural sugar as a pick-me-up. For lunch and dinner, go with more fibrous produce that takes somewhat longer to digest, so you don't suffer that mid-afternoon slump or before-bed craving.

Finally, avoid adding high-calorie or high-fat flavor boosters, such as sugar, plain protein, or full-fat yogurt to your smoothies.

Try using your produce on their own—you may be surprised at just how good they taste naturally.

Without further ado, here are some amazing smoothie recipes to help you lose weight and look great without feeling like you're starving!

The Dish on Negative-Calorie Foods

The Good: *Foods such as tomatoes, cucumbers, celery, lettuce, cabbage, onions, and greens actually require more calories to prepare, eat, digest, and eliminate than they contain. You already know that these foods are nutritious, but now you know that you can eat them in basically unlimited amounts to help you feel full.*

The Bad: *You still need to incorporate foods that contain carbs and protein to give your body what it needs to function properly, make energy, keep your brain going, and protect you from disease. Plus, if you're not getting enough calories, your body will think you're starving and will lower your metabolic rate, making it much more difficult to squeeze back into those skinny jeans!*

Cabbage Soup Smoothie

Rich in vegetables that help your body flush toxins, this drink is both delicious and nutritious. Since it's nutrient dense, you can actually fast with this for a few days, if you so choose to really clean your system out.

- 1/4 head green cabbage
- 1 clove garlic, peeled
- 6–8 basil leaves
- 1 tomato
- 1 green bell pepper, de-stemmed

Blend ingredients well and enjoy.

Yield: About 2 cups.

Skinny Salsa Sauce

Made with many of the same vegetables you find in salsa, this pleasant-tasting juice is low in calories and excellent for cleansing and detoxifying your entire system, so your metabolism can function efficiently. The large amounts of chlorophyll help increase your oxygen use, so your body can drop unhealthful excess weight more quickly.

- 2 green onions
- 1/4 pound wheatgrass
- 2 sprigs cilantro
- 2 tomatoes
- 1 lime, peeled
- 1/2 cup water

Blend all ingredients in the order listed.

Yield: About 2 cups.

Vegetable Soup Smoothie

Anyone who's ever tried to drop a pound—or twenty—has heard of the vegetable soup diet. A delicious play on that concept, this smoothie works especially well as a mini-fast to jump-start your dieting efforts. The cayenne gives it an extra metabolism-boosting kick.

- 1 potato
- 1 green onion
- 2 tomatoes
- 1 green bell pepper, de-stemmed
- 1/4 teaspoon black pepper
- 1 pinch of cayenne pepper

Cut the potato into 1-inch pieces.

Blend ingredients together well.

Yield: About 3 cups.

Perfect Pepper Picker-Upper

Greens are an excellent source of chlorophyll as well as B vitamins for energy and minerals that can help suppress food cravings. Capsaicin from the jalapeño may help burn fat, too. This peppery yet refreshing drink will have you skinny in no time!

- 1/2 jalapeño pepper, de-stemmed
- 1 green bell pepper, de-stemmed
- 1 cucumber, quartered
- 1 cup arugula
- 1/2 cup water

Blend ingredients well.

Yield: About 2 cups.

Skinny Spaghetti in a Glass

This smoothie will remind you of a delicious spaghetti sauce because of the basil and tomato combination. It's a pleasant drink that will help keep you full while providing a potent burst of nutrition.

- 1 clove garlic
- 1 green bell pepper, de-stemmed
- 6 basil leaves
- 2 ripe tomatoes

Blend ingredients well. Add a pinch of sea salt if you'd like.

Yield: About 3 cups.

Southwest Slim-down Gazpacho

Hearty vegetables that are low in calories but high in fiber will help satisfy you and keep you full while assisting you in reaching your weight-loss goals. The Southwest flavors blend together to lend the gazpacho a tasty kick that's sure to be a hit.

- 2 tomatoes
- 2 sprigs cilantro, plus extra for garnish
- 1 green onion
- 1 jalapeño pepper, de-stemmed
- 1 clove garlic
- 1/4 lime, peeled, plus extra for garnish

Since this is a soup, feel free to leave it a bit chunky if you like. You can control the spiciness by removing the seeds of the jalapeño, or if you'd rather, replace it with a green, sweet pepper. Simply blend all ingredients together, and serve in a bowl. Garnish with a sprig of cilantro and a lime twist.

Yield: About 2 cups.

Fill-Me-Up Smoothie

Grapefruit has long been associated with weight loss, and research backs it up. A combination of vitamin C and lots of fiber help you burn fat while staying full. The potassium and other minerals in the banana, plum, and spinach help with muscle recovery after a workout. Meanwhile, the fruity taste makes it perfectly suited for breakfast or a snack.

- 1 grapefruit, peeled and seeded
- 1 plum, pitted
- 1 banana, peeled
- 2 cups spinach
- 1/4 cup water

Add all ingredients to the blender and puree. Pour into a cup and enjoy.

Yield: About 3 cups.

The Dish on Grapefruit

The Good: *In addition to the high fiber content that helps keep you feeling full, grapefruits contain naringenin, an antioxidant that tells your liver to break down fat, so it really is good for weight loss.*

The Bad: *Grapefruit juice doesn't offer all the remarkable health benefits of whole grapefruits: though it's still good for you, it's high in sugar and low in fiber and other fat-fighting components found only in the pulp and white inner skin. Grapefruit also negatively interacts with many medications, both prescription and over-the-counter. Make sure you double-check any potential drug interactions before adding grapefruit to your diet.*

Fresh from the Garden

The rich flavors of this smoothie will remind you of a delicious spaghetti sauce, while the nutrients help your body fight fat. The fiber will keep you full until your next meal, and it's nutritious enough to drink more than once per day, because it offers nearly everything your body needs, all in one appetizing glass.

- 1 tomato
- 2 radishes with greens
- 4 basil leaves
- 1 green bell pepper, de-stemmed
- 2 stalks celery
- 1/2 cup water
- 1 pinch sea salt (optional)

Combine all ingredients in your blender and puree. There are so many great flavors here, you may want to leave this a bit chunky to enjoy some of them individually.

Yield: About 2–3 cups.

Lean Greenie

If you've been in the dieting world for more than ten minutes, you've heard about the weight-loss benefits of cabbage and spinach. Toss in an apple to keep the doctor away, some kiwi just for extra vitamin C, and you've got a slightly sweet smoothie that will make you love green eating!

- 1/2 cup water
- 1 cup cabbage
- 2 cups spinach
- 1 green apple, cored and quartered
- 2 kiwis, peeled

Add all ingredients to your blender, two at a time, starting with the water and cabbage and pulsing between additions. Once all ingredients have been added, puree. Pour into a glass and enjoy.

Yield: About 3 cups.

Lanky Limojito

This is a great little recipe if you're looking for a light, refreshing cocktail. Feel free to make it in larger quantities either in your blender or juicer, and sip on it throughout the day. The citrus it contains will help you burn fat, and the high water and fiber content will help keep you full while flushing toxins and fat out of your system. Also, if you're looking for a low-calorie alternative to standard mojito mix, this is it.

- 1 lime, peeled
- 5 mint leaves
- 1 cucumber, quartered

Add all ingredients to your blender and puree. All of these ingredients work well together, so if you'd like to leave this smoothie a bit chunky to enjoy chewing individual flavors, feel free to do so.

Yield: About 2 cups.

CONCLUSION

Whether you're looking for a way to add some nutrition to your daily diet or seeking to learn more about smoothies to begin your first cleanse, you now have some excellent recipes and tips to get you started. Remember, though, to use this as a general guide. Once you get the hang of mixing flavors, feel free to make up your own blends to suit your tastes and health goals.

Throughout the pages of this book, you've learned many of the benefits of smoothies as well as some basic advice on ingredients. If you're going to add ingredients such as protein or milk to your smoothie, keep it organic and use only the highest-quality products. After all, one of the main reasons for adding smoothies to your diet is to improve your health, so you certainly don't want to add artificial preservatives or toxins.

The other reason many of you may choose to incorporate smoothies into your diet is for weight loss. Because fruits and vegetables are naturally low in calories but high in fiber and good nutrients, they're an ideal component of a weight-loss program, and should be included in any healthful diet.

Be careful in the beginning, however, especially if you're smoothie fasting; it's entirely possible you won't take in enough calories to keep you going throughout the day. If you find yourself getting light-headed or lethargic, simply add a few more carbs back into your diet. You may also want to consider throwing an avocado or some cauliflower or Brussels sprouts into your smoothie for the omega-3 fatty acids.

The goal of this book has been to help you incorporate smoothies into your lifestyle. Hopefully, these pages have demystified smoothies for you, answered your questions on flavor and nutrition, and, most important, inspired you to begin your journey to a healthier, leaner you.

CPSIA information can be obtained
at www.ICGtesting.com
Printed in the USA
BVHW071952041021
618112BV00002B/3